THE AUSTRALIAN
Women's Weekly

CAKE
DECORATING

TRIPLE TESTED · FOR YOUR SUCCESS EVERY TIME

CONTENTS

The oven temperatures in this book are for conventional ovens; if you have a fan-forced oven, decrease the oven temperature by 10-20 degrees. A measurement conversion chart appears on the back flap of this book.

Quilted wedding cake cookies

MAKES 18

EQUIPMENT

oven trays

10cm x 10.5cm (4-inch x 4¼-inch) wedding cake cutter

pastry brush

small patchwork cutter trellis

artist's fine paint brush

tweezers

COOKIES

125g (4 ounces) butter

2 eggs

1 teaspoon vanilla extract

⅔ cup (150g) caster (superfine) sugar

1⅓ cups (200g) self-raising flour

1 cup (150g) plain (all-purpose) flour

DECORATIONS

500g (1 pound) ready-made white icing

cornflour (cornstarch)

1 egg white, beaten lightly

2 tablespoons tiny silver cachous

1 For the cookies, have the butter and eggs at room temperature.

2 Beat butter, extract and sugar in small bowl with electric mixer only until combined. Beat in eggs, one at a time; beat only until combined.

3 Transfer mixture to large bowl. Stir in sifted flours, in two batches; mix to a soft dough. Knead dough on floured surface until smooth, cover; refrigerate 30 minutes.

4 Preheat oven to 180°C/375°F. Grease oven trays; line trays with baking paper.

5 Roll dough, in batches, between sheets of baking paper until 5mm (¼-inch) thick (see step 1). Using wedding cake cutter, cut 18 shapes from dough, re-rolling dough as necessary. Place shapes, about 3cm (1¼ inches) apart, on trays. Bake about 10 minutes or until cookies are browned lightly.

6 Stand cookies on trays 5 minutes; lift onto wire racks to cool.

7 Knead ready-made icing on surface dusted with a little cornflour until icing loses its stickiness. Roll icing on cornfloured surface into a 3mm (⅛-inch) thickness. Using wedding cake cutter, cut 18 shapes from icing; re-roll icing as necessary. Cover icing shapes with plastic wrap.

8 Working with one cookie at a time, brush the top of the cookie with egg white. Lift icing shape onto cookie. Using patchwork cutter, press onto icing to make a quilted pattern (see step 2).

9 Dip paint brush into water, wipe brush almost dry, dab onto one join in the quilted pattern (see step 3); use tweezers to position cachous on join. Repeat with remaining cachous. Stand until set.

tip Completed cookies can be made up to 4 weeks ahead; store at room temperature in an airtight container.

Step 1 Roll out dough between sheets of baking paper until 5mm thick. Using the wedding cake cutter, cut 18 shapes from the dough.

Step 2 Brush the cookies with egg white, top with icing shapes. Press patchwork cutter firmly onto the icing to make a quilted pattern.

Step 3 Dip paint brush into water, wipe brush until almost dry. Lightly dab one join at a time with brush then position cachous on join.

Step 1 Cut a small cavity in the cake top using a small pointed vegetable knife. Fill cavity with jam; use a flavour that will complement the cake.

Step 2 Whip the white chocolate ganache in a small bowl with an electric mixer until the ganache is smooth and thick enough to pipe.

Step 3 Half-fill the piping bag with whipped ganache. Start piping from the centre of the cake, covering the top of each cake to make a large swirl.

Sugar confetti cupcakes

MAKES 12

EQUIPMENT

12 plain white paper cases

large piping bag

1cm (½-inch) plain piping tube

CAKE

1 quantity cupcake mixture of choice (page 107)

jam of choice

DECORATIONS

12 plain decorative cupcake wrappers

1½ quantities white chocolate ganache (page 92), whipped (see step 2, page 6)

2 tablespoons sugar confetti

1 Divide cupcake mixture into paper cases; bake cupcakes according to recipe. Stand cakes in pan 5 minutes; turn top-side up onto wire rack to cool.

2 Cut a small cavity in the top of each cake (see step 1); fill with a little jam. Place cakes into cupcake wrappers.

3 Fit piping bag with tube; half-fill bag with ganache. Pipe swirls of ganache on top of each cake (see step 3). Sprinkle ganache with confetti.

tips Cupcakes stale quickly, so it's best to use a fruit or mud cake for the best keeping qualities. The cakes can be made and frozen for about 3 months. Choose the cake you like, then a type of jam, or a thick fruit puree, to match the cake. For example, any berry jam or puree goes well with a chocolate cake. To make a puree: Push fresh or thawed frozen berries through a sieve; sweeten to taste with a little sifted icing sugar, and add a little liqueur, if you like. Make sure you cover the tops of the cakes with the ganache to keep the cakes as fresh as possible. The ganache will keep them sealed and fresh for a day or two. Completed cakes should be stored in a cool or air-conditioned room. Sprinkle confetti over ganache up to half a day before the cupcakes are to be served.

Chocolate box

EQUIPMENT

20cm (8-inch) square wooden cake board (page 90)

medium metal spatula

craft glue

cheese slicer

CAKE

deep 15cm (6-inch) square cake of choice (page 107)

DECORATIONS

1 quantity white chocolate ganache (page 92)

250g (8 ounces) white chocolate Melts

golden yellow food colouring

1.5m (1½ yards) wide ribbon

3 x 180g (5½-ounce) blocks white eating chocolate

1 Trim cake (page 91); secure cake to board (page 91). Spread cake all over with ganache.

2 Cut baking paper into four strips measuring 10cm x 16cm (4-inches x 6½-inches). Melt chocolate Melts in medium heatproof bowl over medium saucepan of simmering water (don't let water touch base of bowl, see page 104). Remove from heat; tint chocolate with a little yellow food colouring.

3 Using spatula, spread chocolate evenly over the baking-paper strips; leave to set for a few minutes, then carefully pick up paper and move to another sheet of baking paper (see step 1) – this neatens the edges. Stand about 5 minutes or until chocolate sets.

4 Peel baking paper away from chocolate panels (see step 2); press panels onto sides of cake. Wrap ribbon around panels; secure ends with glue. Make bow (page 106); secure over ribbon with glue.

5 Place one block of chocolate upside down on bench. Place your hand on the chocolate to warm it slightly. Drag a sharp cheese slicer over the chocolate to make curls (see step 3). Repeat with remaining chocolate to make enough curls to cover and fill the top of the chocolate box. Fill box with chocolate curls.

tips We found that using a cheese slicer is an easy and effective way of making large chocolate curls. The box panels can be completed at least one week ahead; store at a cool room temperature. You can use this recipe as a guide to make the boxes smaller or larger, as required.

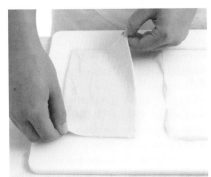

Step 1 To make chocolate panels, spread the melted chocolate over 4 strips of baking paper. When starting to set, lift onto clean baking paper.

Step 2 Stand chocolate at room temperature until it's set. Turn the chocolate over, peel away baking paper, and position the panels around the cake.

Step 3 Place chocolate upside down on bench. Rub your hand over chocolate to warm slightly; drag cheese slicer over chocolate for curls.

Step 1 Using a sharp pointed vegetable knife, gently lift the edge of each monogram off the backing paper then carefully peel away from the paper.

Step 2 Secure monograms to the icing by brushing the backs of the images with a little water. Use the cutter to cut out 12 rounds. Dry overnight.

Step 3 Half-fill the piping bag with ganache. Start piping from the centre of the cakes, covering the top of the cake in a large swirl.

Monogrammed cupcakes

MAKES 12

EQUIPMENT

artist's fine paint brush

3.5cm (1½-inch) round cutter

12 plain white paper cases

large plastic disposable piping bag

CAKE

1 quantity cupcake mixture of choice (page 107)

DECORATIONS

500g (1 pound) ready-made white icing

cornflour (cornstarch)

3cm (1¼-inch) monogrammed edible images

12 fancy cupcake wrappers

1½ quantities dark chocolate ganache (page 92)

1 Knead ready-made icing on surface dusted with a little cornflour until icing loses its stickiness. Roll icing on cornfloured surface into a 3mm (⅛-inch) thickness.

2 Lift 12 monogrammed images off backing paper (see step 1); brush backs of images lightly with a little water; secure to icing about 1cm (½-inch) apart.

3 Use cutter to cut around each image (see step 2); transfer to baking-paper-lined tray to dry overnight.

4 Divide cupcake mixture into paper cases; bake cupcakes according to recipe. Stand cakes in pan 5 minutes; turn top-side up onto wire rack to cool.

5 Secure cupcake wrappers around cakes. Half-fill piping bag with ganache. Cut the tip from the bag; the opening should be about 2cm (¾-inch) wide. Pipe a swirl of ganache onto each cake (see step 3); top with monogrammed rounds.

tips The cupcakes stale quickly so it's best to use a fruit or mud cake for the best keeping qualities. The cakes can be made and frozen for 3 months. The monograms can be prepared at least a month ahead; store them in an airtight container between layers of baking paper. Position the monograms up to half a day before they're needed. Personalise the cupcakes to suit the occasion – there are lots of similar edible images available at cake decorating shops and online. Make sure you cover the tops of the cakes with the ganache to keep the cakes as fresh as possible. The ganache will keep them sealed and fresh for a day or two. Once completed, store the cakes in a cool or air-conditioned room.

Brownie & blondie mini wedding cakes

MAKES 24

EQUIPMENT

2 x 24cm x 32cm (9½-inch x 13-inch) swiss roll pans

5cm (2-inch) round cutter

3.5cm (1½-inch) round cutter

2.5cm (1-inch) round cutter

paper piping bag (page 103)

DARK CHOCOLATE BROWNIE

300g (9½ ounces) dark eating (semi-sweet) chocolate

185g (6 ounces) butter

¼ cup (25g) cocoa powder

1 cup (220g) firmly packed light brown sugar

¾ cup (165g) caster (superfine) sugar

2 teaspoons vanilla extract

4 eggs

1½ cups (225g) plain (all-purpose) flour

WHITE CHOCOLATE BLONDIE

300g (9½ ounces) white eating chocolate

185g (6 ounces) butter

1 cup (220g) caster (superfine) sugar

3 eggs

1¼ cups (185g) plain (all-purpose) flour

⅔ cup (110g) self-raising flour

DECORATIONS

½ quantity dark chocolate ganache (page 92)

2 tablespoons icing (confectioners') sugar

½ teaspoon edible silver glitter

1 Preheat oven to 150°C/300°F. Grease swiss roll pans; line base and long sides with baking paper.

2 Make dark chocolate brownie and white chocolate blondie.

3 Turn blondie and brownie onto board, trim all sides of both cakes (see step 1).

4 Using all of the cutters, cut out 12 rounds of each size from both the brownie and the blondie (see step 2).

5 Make three-tier stacks, alternating rounds of brownies and blondies; pipe a little ganache onto each tier to secure rounds (see step 3).

6 Dust stacks with combined sifted icing sugar and glitter before serving.

dark chocolate brownie Break chocolate into a medium saucepan, add chopped butter and sifted cocoa; stir over low heat until smooth. Cool until just warmed; whisk in sugars, extract, eggs and sifted flour. Spread mixture into one swiss roll pan. Bake about 35 minutes. Cool in pan.

white chocolate blondie Break chocolate into a medium saucepan, add chopped butter; stir over low heat until smooth. Cool until just warmed; whisk in sugar, eggs and sifted flours. Spread mixture into second swiss roll pan. Bake about 35 minutes. Cool in pan.

tips The completed cakes will keep for about 3 days in an airtight container at a cool room temperature, or keep them in the fridge if the weather is hot. The cakes can also be frozen for a month. Dust cakes with sifted icing sugar and glitter just before serving. These miniature wedding cakes would make a lovely gift to hand around to friends at a bridal shower or engagement party.

Step 1 Turn brownie onto a cutting board. Using a long, sharp serrated knife, trim all sides of brownie. Repeat step with the blondie.

Step 2 Using all 3 of the different-sized round cutters, cut out 12 rounds of each size from both the brownie and the blondie.

Step 3 Make three-tier stacks, alternating rounds of brownie and blondie. Pipe a dab of chocolate ganache onto tiers to secure.

Step 1 Using all 3 cutters, cut out rounds from all 4 colours of icing. Keep the icings you're not using airtight by wrapping in plastic wrap.

Step 2 Brush backs of dots lightly with water and randomly position on cake. Don't use too much water or the dots will slip and slide off.

Step 3 Position half-dots around base of the cake. Position dots before they dry so they will more readily take on the contour of the cake.

Polka dots & stripes

EQUIPMENT

4 x 25cm (10-inch) round cake pans

35cm (14-inch) round wooden cake board (page 90)

smoothing tools

2cm (¾-inch), 1.5cm (¾-inch) and 1cm (½-inch) round cutters

artist's fine paint brush

CAKE

4 x 470g (15-ounce) packets butter cake mix

golden yellow, rose pink, mauve and leaf green food colourings

DECORATIONS

4 quantities white chocolate ganache (page 92)

800g (1½ pounds) ready-made white icing

cornflour (cornstarch)

1 Preheat oven to 180°C/360°F. Grease cake pans; line base with baking paper.

2 Make one cake mix according to packet directions. Tint mixture with yellow colouring, spread into pan, bake cake about 30 minutes. Stand cake in pan 5 minutes; turn top-side up onto wire rack to cool. Repeat with remaining cake mixes and pink, mauve and green colouring. Trim cakes level (page 91), if necessary.

3 Secure one cake to board with a little ganache; top with remaining cakes using about ½ cup of the ganache between each layer. Spread cake evenly all over with remaining ganache (page 92).

4 Knead 600g (1¼ pounds) ready-made icing on surface dusted with a little cornflour until icing loses its stickiness. Roll icing on cornfloured surface until large enough to cover cake. Using rolling pin, lift the icing onto cake; smooth with hands then smoothing tools (page 96). Trim icing neatly around base of cake.

5 Knead remaining icing on surface dusted with cornflour until smooth. Divide into 4 equal portions; colour pale pink, green, mauve and yellow. Keep each enclosed in plastic wrap while not using. Roll one colour out into a 1mm (¹⁄₃₂-inch) thickness. Using cutters, cut rounds from icing, re-rolling icing as necessary (see step 1). Repeat with remaining icings. Brush backs of dots sparingly with water (see step 2); position dots on cake (see step 3). Cut some dots in half to decorate around bottom of cake. Dry cake overnight.

tips We used the end of a 1cm piping tube to cut out the smallest dots. If you only have one cake pan, wash then rinse in cold water (to cool the pan), and dry it well between each cake.

Tower of golden macaroons

EQUIPMENT

oven trays

large piping bag

1.5cm (¾-inch) plain piping tube

25cm (10-inch) deep croquembouche mould (diameter 18cm/7¼-inch)

medium-sized ice-cream scoop

25cm (10-inch) round wooden cake board (page 90)

wooden skewer

MACAROONS

6 egg whites

½ cup (110g) caster (superfine) sugar

2½ cups (480g) pure icing (confectioners') sugar

¼ cup (25g) ground almonds

2½ cups (200g) desiccated coconut

CAKE

deep 30cm (12-inch) square coconut cake (page 110)

DECORATIONS

2 quantities white chocolate ganache (page 92), whipped

gold leaf

1   Grease oven trays; line with baking paper.

2   To make macaroons, beat egg whites and caster sugar in medium bowl with electric mixer until soft peaks form and sugar is dissolved.

3   Meanwhile, blend or process icing sugar, ground almonds and coconut until fine and powdery. Sift through fine strainer; discard solids in strainer.

4   Transfer egg white mixture into large bowl. Fold in almond mixture in two batches.

5   Fit large piping bag with tube. Half-fill bag with macaroon mixture. Pipe 50 x 2cm (¾-inch) rounds about 2cm (¾-inch) apart onto trays. Pipe 50 x 3.5cm (1½-inch) rounds about 2cm (¾-inch) apart onto trays. Pipe 50 x 4.5cm (1¾-inch) rounds about 2cm (¾-inch) apart onto trays. Refill bag with macaroon mixture as needed. Tap trays on bench so macaroons spread slightly (see step 1, page 19). Stand macaroons for about 1 hour or until they feel dry to touch (see step 2, page 19).

6   Preheat oven to 120°C/250°F.

7   Bake small macaroons, in batches, about 15 minutes. Cool on trays. Bake remaining macaroons, in batches, about 20 minutes. Cool on trays.

8   Line inside the croquembouche mould with plastic wrap.

9   Cut a 5cm (2-inch) and a 17cm (6¾-inch) round from the coconut cake (see step 3, page 19). Place the small round of cake inside croquembouche mould. Use the ice-cream scoop to scoop rounds of cake (see step 4, page 19); chop remaining cake coarsely.

10 Using half the ganache, pack the mould with a random mix of cake and dollops of ganache. Top with the large round of cake; press down firmly. Refrigerate tower for 3 hours or overnight until firm.

11 Secure cake tower to board with a little ganache (page 92); remove the croquembouche mould. Remove plastic wrap (see step 5, page 19); spread tower all over with remaining ganache.

12 Using a skewer, gently push small pieces of gold leaf onto macaroons (see step 6, page 19). Gently press large macaroons around bottom of the cake, followed by the medium macaroons, then the small macaroons at the top.

Continues overleaf

Continues from previous page

Step 1 Pipe macaroons on baking-paper-lined oven trays. Tap trays firmly several times on bench so macaroons spread a little.

Step 2 Macaroons must feel dry and develop a "skin" before baking; this takes up to an hour depending on the temperature and humidity.

Step 3 Cut a 5cm and 17cm round from the coconut cake. Push a cake pan or plate firmly into the cake to leave a mark to use as a guide.

Step 4 Scoop out rounds from some of the leftover cake using the ice-cream scoop. Coarsely chop the remaining cake scraps.

Step 5 Remove mould; secure tower to board with a little ganache. Remove plastic wrap; spread tower all over with remaining ganache.

Step 6 Gently transfer small pieces of gold leaf onto macaroons. Avoid over-handling the gold leaf as it will stick to your fingers.

tips You can make the macaroons in 2 or 3 batches, if you prefer – base the proportions on 2 or 3 egg whites (either a third or half of the recipe ingredients) and use a small bowl for beating the egg whites and sugar mixture. Ovens are often inaccurate at low temperatures, so reduce the oven temperature if the macaroons are browning. The tower of cake can be made at least a week ahead, and frozen or refrigerated. The ganache coating and macaroons should be positioned on the day of serving.

Gold leaf is delicate and fiddly to handle, but worth the effort. The coconut cake can be kept at room temperature in an airtight container for a week, or may also be frozen for up to 2 months. Choose the best macaroons for the tower. Leftovers will keep in an airtight container at room temperature for at least a week, or can be frozen for about 6 weeks.

Although this tower of macaroons is easy to make – it is time consuming. However, the cake and macaroons can be made well ahead of when the tower is needed. Make sure you have room in the fridge for the cake to set. You need to make about 150 macaroons (we made extra in case of breakages), so it is probably easier to make them in 2-3 batches – make sure you have plenty of oven trays. Draw circles the size of the macaroons onto the back of the baking paper to use as a guide when piping the rounds.

Pink velvet macaroon cake

EQUIPMENT

deep 22cm (9-inch) round cake pan

deep 15cm (6-inch) round cake pan

30cm (12-inch) round wooden cake board (page 90)

15cm (6-inch) round wooden cake board (page 90)

medium offset metal spatula

3 wooden cake skewers

ROSE PINK VELVET CAKE

250g (8 ounces) butter

4 eggs

2 teaspoons vanilla extract

3 cups (660g) caster (superfine) sugar

3 cups (450g) plain (all-purpose) flour

⅓ cup (50g) cornflour (cornstarch)

⅓ cup (35g) cocoa powder

2 cups (500ml) buttermilk

2 tablespoons rose pink food colouring

2 teaspoons white vinegar

2 teaspoons bicarbonate of soda (baking soda)

CREAM CHEESE FROSTING

185g (6 ounces) butter, softened

500g (1 pound) cream cheese, softened

2 tablespoons strained lemon juice

9 cups (1.4kg) icing (confectioners') sugar

DECORATIONS

3 x 114g (3½ ounce) packets small french macaroons

1 Have butter and eggs at room temperature for cake.

2 Preheat oven to 180°C/350°F. Grease and line cake pans (page 88).

3 To make cake, beat butter, eggs, extract and sugar in small bowl with electric mixer until mixture is light and fluffy. Transfer mixture to large bowl; stir in sifted flour, cornflour and cocoa, and the combined buttermilk and colouring, in two batches.

4 Combine vinegar and soda in small bowl; allow to fizz, then fold into cake mixture. Divide mixture between pans. Bake large cake about 1 hour 20 minutes and small cake about 1 hour.

5 Stand cakes in pans 10 minutes; turn top-side up onto wire racks to cool. Wrap cooled cakes in plastic wrap, freeze about 40 minutes or until cakes are firm.

6 Make cream cheese frosting.

7 Trim cakes (page 91). Split large cake into three even layers (see step 1, page 23). Secure one layer to largest board with a little frosting. Top with remaining layers using about ¼ cup of the frosting between each layer.

8 Split smaller cake into three even layers. Secure one layer to small board with a little frosting. Top with the remaining layers using about ¼ cup of the frosting between each layer. Use spatula to spread remaining frosting over top and sides of both cakes (see step 4, page 23).

9 Push trimmed skewers into large cake to support the top tier (page 94). Position small cake on large cake. Smooth frosting with spatula.

10 Gently twist each macaroon to separate into two halves (or carefully cut with a small sharp knife if they're firmly stuck, see step 5, page 23); press the macaroon halves around the sides of both cakes before the frosting sets (see step 6, page 23).

cream cheese frosting Beat the butter, cream cheese and juice in a large bowl with an electric mixer until light and fluffy (see step 2, page 23). Gradually beat in sifted icing sugar (see step 3, page 23) until frosting is smooth.

Continues overleaf

Step 1 Wrap the cakes in plastic wrap and freeze for about 40 minutes or until the cakes are firm. Split each cake into three even layers.

Step 2 To make frosting, have the cream cheese and butter at room temperature. Beat butter, cream cheese and lemon juice until combined.

Step 3 Gradually beat in the sifted icing sugar until the frosting is smooth. Scrape down the sides of the bowl to incorporate the icing sugar.

Step 4 Using a spatula, spread the frosting evenly all over the top and sides of cakes. Smooth frosting after positioning the smaller cake.

Step 5 Gently twist macaroons to separate into two halves or, if they're firmly stuck, carefully cut through the centre with a small sharp knife.

Step 6 Gently press the macaroon halves around the sides of both cakes. Arrange the macaroons in any colour combination you like.

tips We bought packaged macaroons from a supermarket (they are available from the refrigerated section), but you can make your own (see page 17, *Tower of Golden Macaroons* and halve the recipe); you need about 70 single macaroons. Homemade macaroons will keep well in the freezer for about 2 months. This cake freezes well, filled or unfilled. It's at its best assembled on the day of serving.

Bright little jelly bean cakes

EQUIPMENT

2 x 10cm (4-inch) round cardboard cake boards
(page 90)

10cm (4-inch) round wooden cake board (page 90)

2 x 12cm (4¾-inch) round wooden cake boards
(page 90)

6 wooden cake skewers

CAKE

3 x deep 10cm (4-inch) round cakes of choice
(page 107)

2 x deep 12cm (5-inch) round cakes of choice
(page 107)

DECORATIONS

2 quantities butter cream (page 100)

rose pink, leaf green and yellow food colouring

200g (6½ ounces) jelly beans, approximately, in
colours to match the butter cream

1   Divide butter cream evenly into three medium bowls;
tint pink, green and yellow.

2   Trim cakes (page 91). Secure two 10cm cakes to the
10cm cardboards with a little butter cream (see step 1).
Secure the remaining 10cm cake to the 10cm wooden
board. Secure the two 12cm cakes to the 12cm boards.

3   Push 3 trimmed skewers into both 12cm cakes to
support the top tiers (see step 2).

4   Secure the two 10cm cakes on the cardboards to the
12cm cakes (see step 3). You will have 2 x two-tiered
cakes and 1 x one-tier cake.

5   Spread cakes all over with butter cream. Using picture
as a guide, decorate cakes with jelly beans to match the
colours of the butter cream.

tips   Use ganache instead of butter cream, if you
prefer. Once the cakes are covered in butter cream
or ganache, they will keep for about a week at a
cool room temperature. The jelly beans can be
placed on the cakes as soon as the butter cream
has been applied.
These quirky little cakes are so easy to make, and
are ideal for baby showers. Mix and match the
colours and flavours of the jelly beans and the
butter cream to suit the occasion.

Step 1 Secure two 10cm cakes to the 10cm cardboards with a little butter cream. Secure the remaining 10cm cake to the 10cm wooden board.

Step 2 Using a sharp serrated knife, trim skewers to the height of the cake (page 94). Push skewers into the largest cakes to support the top tiers.

Step 3 Once all cakes are on boards, secure two of the smaller cakes onto the larger cakes with a little of the butter cream.

Embossed lace cupcakes

MAKES 12

EQUIPMENT

12 plain white paper cases

texture-embossing mat

7cm (2¾-inch) round cutter

new large soft-bristled brush

CAKE

1 quantity cupcake mixture of choice (page 107)

DECORATIONS

1 quantity white chocolate ganache (page 92)

500g (1 pound) ready-made white icing

cornflour (cornstarch)

12 fancy cupcake wrappers

food-grade white shimmer

1   Divide cupcake mixture into paper cases; bake cupcakes according to recipe. Stand cakes in pan 5 minutes; turn top-side up onto wire rack to cool.

2   Spread tops of cakes evenly all over with ganache.

3   Knead ready-made icing on surface dusted with a little cornflour until icing loses its stickiness. Roll icing on cornfloured surface into a 5mm (¼-inch) thickness.

4   Place textured mat on top of the icing, using a rolling pin, firmly press and roll pattern onto icing (see step 1). Carefully remove mat (see step 2). Using cutter, cut out 12 rounds from icing; carefully place rounds on cakes without touching the embossed pattern (see step 3). Knead and re-roll the icing and cut out more rounds as needed.

5   Carefully place cakes into cupcake wrappers. Dip brush into shimmer; brush lightly over embossed pattern.

tips   Ensure you have enough cakes for all the guests. If you like, choose a few different cake recipes, so you get a variety of cakes. The ganache and ready-made icing covering will keep the cakes fresh for a few days in a cool or air-conditioned room. Apply the shimmer to the icing a few hours before serving; a clean soft-bristled make-up brush is ideal for doing this.
Display these elegant little cakes on a cake stand to show them off. We used patterned cupcake wrappers to hide the plain paper cases.

Step 1 Roll the soft icing until 5mm thick on a cornfloured surface. Use rolling pin to press textured mat into icing to make pattern.

Step 2 Carefully remove the textured mat from the patterned icing to prevent tearing and damaging the embossed pattern.

Step 3 Cut out rounds from the embossed icing; carefully position on ganache-topped cakes to prevent marking the pattern.

Lemon meringue cupcakes

MAKES 12

EQUIPMENT

12 straight-sided fancy paper cases

oven tray

large piping bag

2cm (¾-inch) plain piping tube

craft glue

CAKE

1 quantity cupcake mixture of choice (page 107)

MERINGUES

2 egg whites

½ cup (110g) caster (superfine) sugar

lemon yellow food colouring

DECORATIONS

1 cup (320g) lemon curd

3m (3 yards) narrow ribbon

1 Divide cupcake mixture into paper cases; bake cupcakes according to recipe. Stand cakes in pan 5 minutes; turn top-side up onto wire rack to cool.

2 Reduce oven temperature to 100°C/210°F. Grease and line oven tray with baking paper (see tips).

3 To make meringues, beat egg whites and sugar in small bowl with electric mixer until sugar is dissolved and mixture is thick and glossy. Tint meringue pale yellow with colouring.

4 Fit piping bag with tube, half-fill bag with meringue; pipe 12 meringues, with bases 5cm (2 inches) wide, onto oven tray, about 5cm apart (see step 1), refilling bag as necessary. Bake meringues about 45 minutes or until dry to touch. Cool in oven with door ajar.

5 Trim tops from cakes so the tops are flat and 1cm (½ inch) below the top of the paper cases. Spread one tablespoon of curd over each cake to completely cover the surface of the cake. Top cakes with meringues (see step 2).

6 Position a length of ribbon around each cake; secure ends with glue. Use ribbon to make bows (page 106); secure over joins with glue (see step 3).

tips Use a 5cm (2-inch) round cutter to draw circles on baking paper about 5cm apart. Turn the paper over and use circles as a guide to pipe the meringues. Cakes can be frozen for up to 3 months. Meringues can be made a week ahead and stored in an airtight container at a cool room temperature. Assemble the cakes up to a day before needed.

Step 1 Pipe meringues onto the oven tray. If you like, draw 5cm circles, 5cm apart, on the baking paper as a guide; turn paper over before piping.

Step 2 Trim tops from the cakes so they are about 1cm below the top of the paper cases to make room for the curd and meringue.

Step 3 Using craft glue, secure a length of ribbon around the cakes. Cover the ribbon ends with small bows secured with glue.

Step 1 Using base of the springform pan, cut out two sponge rounds close to the edge. Use scraps to complete second sponge round.

Step 2 You need mangoes that are ripe, but firm enough to slice thinly. Peel mangoes, remove seed, then slice the cheeks thinly.

Step 3 Starting from the cheesecake centre, and using small slices of mango for the bud, arrange mango slices into a rose shape.

Mango rose cheesecakes

MAKES 4

EQUIPMENT

4 x 10cm (4-inch) (closed) springform pans

CHEESECAKE

250g (8 ounces) cream cheese

1 x 450g (14½ ounce) unfilled store-bought sponge slab (13cm x 18cm) (5¼-inch x 7¼-inch)

1 teaspoon powdered gelatine

2 teaspoons finely grated lime rind

2 tablespoons lime juice

¼ cup (55g) caster (superfine) sugar

1 cup (250ml) pouring cream

DECORATION

2 medium firm ripe mangoes (860g)

1 Have cream cheese at room temperature.

2 Split sponge cake into two even layers. Using base of one springform pan as a guide, cut out four rounds of sponge (see step 1). Use scraps of sponge to patch and complete rounds, as necessary.

3 Line base and sides of springform pans with baking paper. Place sponge rounds into pans.

4 To make cheesecake: Sprinkle gelatine over juice in small heatproof jug. Stand 5 minutes then place jug in small saucepan of simmering water, stir until gelatine is dissolved. Cool 5 minutes.

5 Beat cream cheese, rind and sugar in small bowl with electric mixer until smooth; beat in cream. Stir in gelatine mixture.

6 Divide cream cheese mixture evenly between pans; level tops. Refrigerate overnight.

7 Remove cheesecakes from pans, place on serving plates. Slice mango into 3mm (⅛-inch) thick slices (see step 2). Starting from the centre of cheesecake, and using small pieces of mango first, arrange slices into a rose shape (see step 3).

tips Everybody loves their own individual dessert – here, the tropical flavours blend happily with the creamy cheesecake filling. The mango rose pattern is simple to achieve, but looks impressive on the cheesecakes. We used a plain store-bought sponge for this recipe; you can make your own if you like. The cheesecakes are at their best made one day ahead; keep refrigerated.

Coconut dream cream cake

EQUIPMENT

45cm (18-inch) round wooden cake board (page 90)

25cm (10-inch) round wooden cake board (page 90)

20cm (8-inch) round wooden cake board (page 90)

15cm (6-inch) round wooden cake board (page 90)

10cm (4-inch) round wooden cake board (page 90)

12 wooden cake skewers

small offset metal spatula

CAKE

deep 30cm (12-inch) round cake of choice (page 107)

deep 25cm (10-inch) round cake of choice (page 107)

deep 20cm (8-inch) round cake of choice (page 107)

deep 15cm (6-inch) round cake of choice (page 107)

deep 10cm (4-inch) round cake of choice (page 107)

DECORATIONS

3 quantities white chocolate ganache (page 92)

white food colouring

1.8kg (3½ pounds) ball-shaped coconut chocolates

1 Trim cakes (page 91). Secure largest cake to largest board (page 91). Secure the remaining cakes to the same-sized boards.

2 Push 3 trimmed skewers into centre of each cake, except the smallest cake, to support the next tier (page 94).

3 Assemble cakes, securing each tier to the tier below (page 94).

4 Beat ganache in a large bowl with an electric mixer (see step 1). Beat in enough white colouring to match the colour of the ganache to the coconut chocolates. Using spatula, spread cake all over with ganache (see step 2).

5 Cut chocolates in half (see step 3); starting at the bottom of the largest cake, press the cut-sides of the chocolates around each cake to cover.

tips The cake can be completed a day ahead. It will be fine kept in a cool or air-conditioned room. Instead of making the ganache, you could buy 3 x 453g (16-ounce) tubs of vanilla frosting to cover this cake.

This is an easy cake to make and decorate; use any cake you like – we prefer a white chocolate mud cake (page 112) or a coconut cake (page 110). Whichever type you choose, the cake will be heavy to move and lift, so get someone to help.

Step 1 Beat ganache in a large bowl with an electric mixer. Use white colouring to match the colour of the ganache to the chocolates.

Step 2 Secure and stack cakes together. Using a small metal spatula, spread ganache evenly all over the cake to make it airtight.

Step 3 Using a sharp knife, cut the coconut chocolates in half. Starting from the bottom of the cake, push cut sides of chocolates onto ganache to cover the cake.

Coconut ruffle cake

EQUIPMENT

40cm (16-inch) round wooden cake board (page 90)

30cm (12-inch) round wooden cake board (page 90)

25cm (10-inch) round wooden cake board (page 90)

20cm (8-inch) round wooden cake board (page 90)

15cm (6-inch) round wooden cake board (page 90)

12 wooden cake skewers

medium offset metal spatula

CAKE

deep 35cm (14-inch) round cake of choice (page 107)

deep 30cm (12-inch) round cake of choice (page 107)

deep 25cm (10-inch) round cake of choice (page 107)

deep 20cm (8-inch) round cake of choice (page 107)

deep 15cm (6-inch) round cake of choice (page 107)

DECORATIONS

5 quantities white chocolate ganache (page 92)

white food colouring

1kg (2 pounds) flaked coconut

1 Trim cakes (page 91). Secure largest cake to largest board with a little ganache (page 91). Secure remaining cakes to same-sized boards.

2 Push 3 trimmed skewers into centres of all cakes, except the smallest cake, to support the next tier (page 94).

3 Assemble cake, securing each tier to the tier below (page 94).

4 Place half the ganache in a large bowl; whisk in at least 1 tablespoon of white colouring until the ganache is as white as possible (see step 1). Beat ganache with an electric mixer until light and fluffy (see step 2). Repeat with remaining ganache.

5 Using spatula, spread cake all over with ganache. Gently press handfuls of the flaked coconut all over the cake (see step 3).

tips We used flaked coconut labelled 'coconut chipped' found in health food stores. Instead of making the ganache you could buy 5 x 453g (16-ounce) tubs of vanilla frosting to cover this cake. The cake can be assembled completely a week before it's required; it will be fine kept in a cool or air-conditioned room. Use any cake recipe you like: our favourite is the coconut cake (page 110). This five tier cake is very heavy to move and lift, so get someone to help you.

Step 1 Place half the ganache in a large bowl. Whisk at least 1 tablespoon of food colouring into the ganache to whiten the colour as much as possible.

Step 2 Beat half the ganache at a time in large bowl with electric mixer until light and fluffy, scrape down side of bowl during beating.

Step 3 Once the cake is covered with the ganache, firmly press handfuls of coconut all over the cake. Choose long flakes for the top tier.

Hearts & bows forever

EQUIPMENT

3cm (1¼-inch) heart cutter

22cm (9-inch) round wooden cake board (page 90)

small offset metal spatula

CAKE

2 x deep 18cm (7-inch) round cakes of choice (page 107)

DECORATIONS

150g (4½ ounces) ready-made white icing

cornflour (cornstarch)

lemon yellow food colouring

1½ quantities white chocolate ganache (page 92)

1m (1 yard) wide ribbon

1   Knead ready-made icing on surface dusted with a little cornflour until icing loses its stickiness. Tint icing yellow with colouring. Roll icing out on cornfloured surface into a 3mm (⅛-inch) thickness.

2   Using cutter, cut out about 70 heart shapes from icing (see step 1), re-rolling scraps as necessary. Place hearts on a baking-paper-lined tray for about 3 hours, or until hearts are firm, but not dried out or hard.

3   Trim cakes (page 91). Secure one cake to board; top with remaining cake, joining cakes with a little ganache (page 92).

4   Beat remaining ganache in small bowl with electric mixer until light and fluffy.

5   Using spatula, spread ganache all over cake (see step 2).

6   Starting from the bottom of the cake, press hearts into ganache in rows before the ganache sets (see step 3).

7   Just before serving, decorate the top of the cake with a bow made from the ribbon (page 106).

tip   If you prefer, use butter cream instead of ganache; both will keep the cake airtight and fresh for at least a week in a cool or air-conditioned room.

Step 1 Cut out 70 heart shapes from the icing; place on a baking-paper-lined tray until firm, but not dried out or hard.

Step 2 Secure one cake to board; top with remaining cake, secure with ganache. Spread cake evenly all over with remaining ganache.

Step 3 Starting from the bottom of the cake, gently press the heart shapes in rows around the cake. Do this before the ganache sets.

Step 1 Using a ruler and sharp knife, cut transfer sheets into 3 rectangles large enough to cover the cake. Reserve any transfer scraps.

Step 2 Cover cake with chocolate-covered transfer sheet; stand 20 minutes, then carefully peel the backing paper away from the transfer.

Step 3 Coat the transfer sheet with chocolate; remove backing paper when dry, then use both the fluted cutters to cut rounds from transfers.

White chocolate rose-print cake

MAKES 3

EQUIPMENT

3 x 10cm (4-inch) round cardboard cake boards
(page 90)

small offset metal spatula

plastic ruler

tape measure

4.5cm (1¾-inch) fluted round cutter

3.5cm (1½-inch) fluted round cutter

CAKE

3 x 10cm (4-inch) round cakes of choice (page 107)

DECORATIONS

1½ quantities white chocolate ganache (page 92)

2 x 25cm x 40cm (10-inch x 16-inch) chocolate
transfer sheets

750g (1½ pounds) white chocolate Melts

2m (2 yards) wide ribbon

1 Trim cakes (page 91). Secure cakes to boards (page 91). Using spatula, spread cakes all over using two-thirds of the ganache (page 92).

2 Using tape measure, measure the circumference and height of the cakes and add 1cm (½ inch) to each of these measurements. Using a ruler and a sharp knife, cut 3 rectangles from the transfer sheets using these measurements (see step 1). Reserve any leftover transfer sheet scraps.

3 Melt chocolate in medium bowl over medium saucepan of simmering water (don't allow water to touch base of bowl, see page 104). Place one cut transfer sheet, print-side up, on a clean surface. Using spatula, spread sheet with one-third of the melted chocolate. Chocolate should be 3mm (⅛-inch) thick to make it easy to handle. Leave chocolate to set for a few minutes, then carefully pick up transfer sheet and move to a sheet of baking paper (this neatens the edges). While the chocolate is still wet to the touch, and before the edges have begun to set, carefully pick up the top two corners and wrap the transfer sheet around one cake, chocolate-side in. Repeat with the remaining transfer sheets, chocolate and cakes. Stand 20 minutes then remove the backing paper. To remove the backing paper, start from one top corner and carefully peel paper away (see step 2).

4 Spread remaining chocolate over any leftover pieces of transfer sheet; leave to set completely before removing the backing paper. Using both fluted cutters, cut out rounds from sheet (see step 3). Top cakes with remaining ganache, then chocolate rounds. Tie ribbon around cake, finish with a bow (page 106).

tips Cakes can be completed at least a week before required. Store in a cool or air-conditioned room. Position the fluted chocolate rounds on top of the cake on the day of serving.

Meringue cloud cake

EQUIPMENT

oven trays

medium offset metal spatula

large piping bag

7.5mm (¼-inch) plain piping tube

30cm (12-inch) round wooden cake board (page 90)

15cm (6-inch) round wooden cake board (page 90)

3 wooden cake skewers

craft glue

MERINGUE

8 egg whites

2 cups (440g) caster (superfine) sugar

2 tablespoons cornflour (cornstarch)

2 teaspoons white vinegar

CAKE

deep 20cm (8-inch) round cake of choice (page 107)

deep 15cm (6-inch) round cake of choice (page 107)

DECORATIONS

300ml (½ pint) thickened (heavy) cream

125g (4 ounces) fresh raspberries

50cm (20 inches) wide ribbon

1   Preheat oven to 120°C/250°F. Line oven trays with baking paper. Mark an 18cm (7¼-inch) circle on one tray; turn paper over. Mark 9cm (3¾-inch) straight lines (you need about 100) on remaining trays; turn paper over.

2   To make meringue: Beat egg whites in large bowl with electric mixer until soft peaks form; gradually add sugar, beat until dissolved between additions. Beat in sifted cornflour, then vinegar. Using spatula, spread half the mixture inside circle on tray. Shape sides up and in towards the centre (see step 1). Bake large meringue about 1 hour, or until dry to touch. Remove from oven; cool on tray.

3   Fit piping bag with tube. Half-fill bag with meringue; pipe about 100 x 9cm finger-width meringue sticks, about 2cm (¾ inch) apart, on remaining oven trays (see step 2). Refill bag as necessary. Bake the sticks about 30 minutes or until dry to touch. Remove from oven; cool on trays.

4   Beat cream in small bowl with electric mixer until firm peaks form; cover, refrigerate until ready to use.

5   Trim cakes (page 91). Secure large cake to largest board; secure small cake to small board. Push trimmed skewers into large cake to support top tier (page 94). Secure small cake on top of large cake. Spread cakes all over with cream.

6   Position meringue sticks around sides of both cakes. Scoop out large spoonfuls of meringue (see step 3); place between the tiers and on the top of small cake.

7   Sprinkle cake with raspberries. Wrap ribbon around large cake, secure ends with glue.

tips   If short on oven space, halve the meringue recipe and make the large meringue and the sticks separately. The cake can be assembled and covered with cream one day ahead; store in the refrigerator. Arrange the meringue sticks and spoonfuls of soft meringue as close to serving as possible. Meringues will soften in about 1 hour.

You can buy sponge cakes for this recipe, if you like (preferably jam and cream filled). You could also buy a large meringue as well, to break up and use to fill and decorate the cake. In this case, you'll need half the meringue ingredients only, to make the meringue sticks. Meringue sticks can be made a month ahead; store in an airtight container at a cool room temperature. Make the large meringue the day before required.

Step 1 Mark an 18cm circle on baking paper, invert onto an oven tray. Spread meringue inside circle, and shape inwards and upwards.

Step 2 Fit piping bag with tube. Pipe finger lengths of meringue, using markings as a guide, onto the baking-paper-covered trays.

Step 3 Avoiding browned or caramelised meringue, scoop out large tablespoons of soft meringue onto top of cake and around top of large cake.

Chocolate box of hearts

EQUIPMENT

22cm (9-inch) round or heart-shaped wooden cake board (page 90)

small offset metal spatula

straight-sided metal scraper

paper piping bag (page 103)

cheese slicer

CAKE

1 heart-shaped cake of choice (page 107)

DECORATIONS

1 quantity white chocolate ganache (page 92) (see method step 1, below)

1 tablespoon instant coffee granules

370g (12 ounces) white chocolate Melts

1 x 180g (5½-ounce) block white eating chocolate

15 heart-shaped chocolates, approximately

2m (2 yards) wide ribbon

1 Make the white chocolate ganache, add coffee granules to the cream while heating; stir until smooth.

2 Trim cake (page 91). Secure cake to board with a little ganache.

3 Use spatula to spread cake all over with ganache until it is about 1cm (½-inch) thick. Stand cake about 20 minutes or until ganache becomes slightly firmer. Using metal scraper, scrape excess ganache from top and side of cake (see step 1, page 45). Reserve ganache scrapings in a small bowl; cover with plastic wrap.

4 Using a small knife, cut a 2cm (¾-inch) deep line right around the cake, 1cm (½ inch) in from edge of cake (see step 2, page 45). Refrigerate cake 3 hours or overnight.

5 Scoop out cake (with ganache) inside the cut line to make a recess in the cake about 2cm deep (see step 3, page 45); discard scrapings. Warm reserved ganache over a small saucepan of simmering water; spread ganache evenly inside the recess – don't fill the recess with the ganache, just use it to cover the base and sides (see step 4, page 45).

6 Trace around base of heart-shaped cake pan onto baking paper to make a template for the chocolate box lid. Turn paper over onto a flat tray.

7 Melt chocolate Melts in a small heatproof bowl over small saucepan of simmering water (don't let water touch base of bowl – page 104). Three-quarters fill piping bag with chocolate, snip end from bag; pipe a thick band of chocolate inside the heart outline. Spread more chocolate in the centre of the heart (see step 5, page 45); stand about 10 minutes or until chocolate is set. Repeat this process using remaining chocolate to make a thick lid; re-melt chocolate as necessary.

8 Turn the block of white chocolate upside down; rub your hand over the chocolate to soften slightly. Drag the blade of the cheese slicer over the flat surface of the chocolate to make curls. Position chocolates in box; sprinkle curls between chocolates.

9 Peel baking paper from the back of the chocolate lid (see step 6, page 45); tie a ribbon around lid, finish with a bow (page 106). Place on top of cake.

Continues overleaf

Step 1 Use a straight-sided metal scraper to smooth the side and top of the heart. Reserve all the ganache scrapings in a small bowl.

Step 2 Using a small sharp knife, cut a 2cm deep line around the cake leaving a 1cm border. Refrigerate cake 3 hours or overnight.

Step 3 Using a large spoon, scoop out the cake and ganache to make a recess in the cake; discard the cake and ganache scraps.

Step 4 Warm the reserved ganache over simmering water until spreadable. Spread ganache evenly over base and side of recess.

Step 5 Pipe melted chocolate around heart outline; spread more chocolate in the centre of the heart. Repeat to make a thick lid.

Step 6 Allow the chocolate lid to set at room temperature. Carefully remove the heart from the baking paper; place on top of cake.

tips Ganache will keep the cake airtight for at least a week if stored in a cool or air-conditioned room.

A cheese slicer makes curls about 2.5cm (1-inch) long (page 105); if you don't have one, use a vegetable peeler – it will make smaller curls.

We used a white chocolate mud cake (page 112) in this recipe, and made a coffee-flavoured ganache to complement it and the chocolates, however, a dark chocolate mud cake (page 113) would also look wonderful filled with heart-shaped chocolates in red wrappers.

Last-minute cake with fresh flowers

EQUIPMENT

30cm (12-inch) round wooden cake board (page 90)

20cm (8-inch) round wooden cake board (page 90)

15cm (6-inch) round wooden cake board (page 90)

6 wooden cake skewers

small offset metal spatula

CAKE

deep 25cm (10-inch) round cake of choice (page 107)

deep 20cm (8-inch) round cake of choice (page 107)

deep 15cm (6-inch) round cake of choice (page 107)

DECORATIONS

2 quantities fluffy frosting (page 101) (see tips)

fresh organic flowers

white florist's tape

1   Trim cakes (page 91). Secure large cake to largest board; secure remaining cakes to same-sized boards (page 91).

2   Push 3 trimmed skewers into centre of large and medium cakes to support the top tiers (page 94). Secure medium cake on top of large cake; secure small cake on top of medium cake.

3   Make fluffy frosting (see step 1). Working quickly, spread frosting all over cake (see step 2).

4   Trim flower stems, wrap the stems in florist's tape (see step 3). Position flowers on top of cake.

tips   Make the frosting after you have stacked and secured the cakes; you need to work quickly once the frosting is ready as it sets quickly. This frosting colours beautifully if you want a pastel-coloured cake to fit in with the colour theme of your event. The cakes can be frosted one day ahead, however, the frosting loses its sheen once it has set. The flowers should be prepared and positioned on the day of serving.

Step 1 Beat fluffy frosting in a small bowl with an electric mixer until it is thick, spreadable and almost cooled to room temperature.

Step 2 Be ready to spread the frosting onto the cake as soon as it's prepared; you need to work quickly before the frosting sets.

Step 3 On the day of serving, trim flower stems to lie neatly on top of cake. Wrap stems in florist's tape; position flowers on cake.

Autumn leaves

EQUIPMENT

35cm (14-inch) round wooden cake board (page 90)

20cm (8-inch) round wooden cake board (page 90)

15cm (6-inch) round wooden cake board (page 90)

smoothing tools

6 wooden cake skewers

paper piping bag (page 103)

CAKE

deep 25cm (10-inch) round cake of choice (page 107)

deep 20cm (8-inch) round cake of choice (page 107)

deep 15cm (6-inch) round cake of choice (page 107)

DECORATIONS

1.4kg (2¾ pounds) ready-made white icing

cornflour (cornstarch)

orange and brown food colourings

1 quantity royal icing (page 102)

freshly picked organic leaves (see tips)

2m (2 yards) narrow ribbon

1 Trim cakes (page 91). Secure large cake to largest board; secure remaining cakes to the same-sized boards. Prepare cakes for covering with ready-made icing (page 91).

2 Knead ready-made icing on surface dusted with a little cornflour until icing loses its stickiness. Divide icing into three portions: 300g (9½ ounces), 500g (1 pound) and 600g (1¼ pounds).

3 Use both colourings to tint all the icings three different autumnal shades. Colour the largest portion the darkest, the middle portion the palest and the smallest portion a medium shade.

4 Roll the largest portion of icing on cornfloured surface until large enough to cover largest cake. Using rolling pin, lift icing onto cake; smooth with hands then smoothing tools. Trim icing neatly around base of cake. Use medium portion of icing to cover medium cake in the same way as the large cake. Use remaining icing to cover small cake in the same way. Dry cakes overnight.

5 Push 3 trimmed skewers into centres of large and medium cakes to support the next tier (page 94). Assemble cakes, securing each tier to the tier below.

6 Divide royal icing into 3 bowls; tint with colourings to match cakes. Half-fill piping bag with icing; pipe around base of same-coloured cake. Use fingertip to blend icing into any gaps where cakes join the boards (page 94). Dry cakes overnight.

7 Wash leaves carefully in cold water; leave to dry on kitchen paper (see step 1).

8 Wrap and secure ribbon around base of each tier with a dot of royal icing (see step 2). Pipe dots of icing onto backs of leaves; position leaves on cake (see step 3).

tips If you choose leaves other than the Japanese maple, check they're organic and free from toxins. Wash, dry and position leaves as close to serving time as possible (4 hours ahead is fine). Use small dried leaves, if you prefer.

Step 1 Gently wash trimmed leaves in cold water; shake off excess water. Place the leaves on absorbent paper; leave until dry.

Step 2 Measure around each cake, cut ribbon into corresponding lengths. Position ribbon around cakes; join ends with a little royal icing.

Step 3 Position the leaves on the cake. Pipe tiny dots of royal icing onto the back of the leaves to secure to the cake.

Step 1 Roll a little brown icing on surface dusted with a little cornflour. Cut out heart shape. Repeat using some of the ivory icing.

Step 2 Cut the wire in half. Push one piece of wire about halfway into each heart shape. Dry on baking-paper-lined tray overnight.

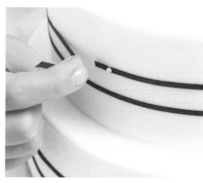

Step 3 Measure and cut ribbons to go around cakes. Secure ribbons to cakes with tiny dots of royal icing. Join the ends with royal icing.

Chocolate & ivory hearts cake

EQUIPMENT

9cm (3¾-inch) heart cutter

20cm (8-inch) 18-gauge floral wire

wire cutters

35cm (14-inch) round wooden cake board (page 90)

20cm (8-inch) round wooden cake board (page 90)

15cm (6-inch) round wooden cake board (page 90)

smoothing tools

6 wooden cake skewers

paper piping bag (page 103)

CAKE

deep 25cm (10-inch) round cake of choice (page 107)

deep 20cm (8-inch) round cake of choice (page 107)

deep 15cm (6-inch) round cake of choice (page 107)

DECORATIONS

1.5kg (3 pounds) ready-made ivory icing

cornflour (cornstarch)

chocolate brown and ivory food colouring

1 quantity royal icing (page 102)

5m (5 yards) narrow ribbon

1 Colour 40g (1½ ounces) ready-made ivory icing chocolate brown; knead on surface dusted with a little cornflour until icing loses its stickiness. Roll icing on cornfloured surface into a 3mm (⅛-inch) thickness. Using cutter, cut a heart shape from icing (see step 1). Cut wire in half, push one half into the heart shape (see step 2); place on baking-paper-lined tray to dry overnight. Make another heart in the same way using 40g of the ready-made ivory icing.

2 Trim cakes (page 91). Secure large cake to largest board; secure remaining cakes to same-sized boards. Prepare cakes for covering with ready-made icing (page 91).

3 Knead remaining ivory icing on surface dusted with a little cornflour until icing loses its stickiness.

4 Roll 300g (9½ ounces) of icing on cornfloured surface until large enough to cover small cake. Using rolling pin, lift icing onto cake; smooth with hands then smoothing tools. Trim icing around base of cake.

5 Use 500g (1 pound) of the icing to cover medium cake in the same way as the small cake. Use remaining icing to cover large cake in the same way. Dry cakes overnight.

6 Push 3 trimmed skewers into centres of large and medium cakes to support the next tier (page 94). Assemble cakes, securing each tier to the tier below.

7 Tint royal icing ivory to match cake. Three-quarters fill piping bag with royal icing; pipe around base of each cake. Use fingertip to blend icing into any gaps where cakes join the boards (page 94). Dry cakes overnight.

8 Cut ribbon in lengths long enough to go around cakes. Secure around cakes using tiny dots of royal icing. Join ends of ribbon with royal icing (see step 3).

9 To position hearts, gently push wires into cake.

tips The hearts can be made weeks ahead; store in an airtight container. Position them on the day of serving. Positioning and securing the ribbon around these cakes can be fiddly, as the ribbon can easily slip out of position. It's best to secure the ribbon after the icing has set completely, which takes about two days.

Cake pop baby rattles

MAKES 18

EQUIPMENT

18 x 30cm (12-inch) cake pop sticks

large square styrofoam block

2 paper piping bags (page 103)

CAKE POPS

4 cups (340g) firmly packed cake crumbs (see tips)

½ quantity butter cream, approximately (page 100)

DECORATION

375g (12 ounces) white chocolate Melts

1 quantity royal icing (page 102)

blue and pink food colouring

1.5m (1½ yards) each blue and pink narrow ribbon

1 Using a fork, combine the cake crumbs and enough (about ½ cup) butter cream in a medium bowl to make ingredients come together.

2 Gently roll level tablespoons of mixture into balls. Place balls on tray; freeze 1 hour or refrigerate 3 hours or overnight.

3 Melt chocolate in medium heatproof bowl over medium saucepan of simmering water until smooth (don't let water touch base of bowl, see page 104). Pour into a heatproof jug.

4 Dip the end of a cake pop stick into the chocolate, then push the stick about halfway into a ball of cake (see step 1). Place in freezer for 5 minutes to set.

5 Make one cake pop rattle at a time: Dip the cake pop in the chocolate, rocking back and forth to coat (see step 2); don't swirl the pops or they'll break. Allow excess chocolate to drip back into the jug. Stand cake pops upright in styrofoam to set at room temperature or in the fridge. Repeat with remaining cake pops. Re-melt the chocolate as necessary (page 104).

6 Divide royal icing into two small bowls, tint one batch pale pink, the other pale blue; cover surface of icing with plastic wrap to keep airtight.

7 Three-quarters fill one piping bag with pink royal icing; pipe spirals on top of half the cake pops (see step 3), turning the cake pops in the styrofoam as you pipe. Repeat with blue royal icing and remaining cake pops. Stand in styrofoam until set.

8 Use the ribbon to tie tiny bows at the base of each cake pop (page 106).

tips Use any firm-textured cake to make cake pops – mud, fruit, coconut or butter cakes all work well. Leftover Christmas cake or pudding are real winners as they're usually moist. Cake pop sticks (also sold as 'lollypop candy sticks') are available from cake decorating suppliers and craft shops. Store cake pops, lying down, in a single layer, in an airtight container at a cool room temperature.

Step 1 Dip the end of a cake pop stick into the melted white chocolate; push the stick about halfway through into the ball of cake.

Step 2 Dip each cake pop in the melted chocolate; rock them back and forth to ensure that they are evenly coated.

Step 3 Pipe spirals of pink and blue royal icing around tops of the cake pops, turning the cake pops in the styrofoam as you pipe.

Pleats & bows ribbon cake

EQUIPMENT

35cm (14-inch) round wooden cake board (page 90)

20cm (8-inch) round wooden cake board (page 90)

15cm (6-inch) round wooden cake board (page 90)

10cm (4-inch) round wooden cake board (page 90)

smoothing tools

19 wooden cake skewers

paper piping bag (page 103)

3.7cm (1½-inch) perspex measure

pizza cutter

artist's fine paint brush

tape measure

CAKE

deep 25cm (10-inch) round cake of choice (page 107)

deep 20cm (8-inch) round cake of choice (page 107)

deep 15cm (6-inch) round cake of choice (page 107)

deep 10cm (4-inch) round cake of choice (page 107)

DECORATIONS

3kg (6 pounds) ready-made white icing

cornflour (cornstarch)

1 quantity royal icing (page 102)

4m (4 yards) narrow ribbon

perspex initials

1 Trim cakes (page 91). Secure 25cm cake to largest board; secure remaining cakes to the same-sized boards. Prepare cakes for covering with ready-made icing (page 91).

2 Knead ready-made icing on surface dusted with a little cornflour until icing loses its stickiness. Roll 300g (9½ ounces) of icing on cornfloured surface until large enough to cover 10cm cake. Using rolling pin, lift icing onto cake; smooth with hands then smoothing tools. Trim icing neatly around base of cake. (Reserve and re-use all icing scraps from each cake for the next cake.)

3 Roll icing on surface dusted with a little cornflour; use 400g (12½ ounces) of icing to cover 15cm cake; 600g (1¼ pounds) to cover 20cm cake; and 700g (1½ pounds) to cover 25cm cake, in the same way as the 10cm cake. Dry cakes overnight.

4 Push 3 trimmed skewers into centres of all cakes, except the smallest cake, to support the next tier (page 94). Assemble cakes, securing each tier to the tier below.

5 Three-quarters fill piping bag with royal icing; pipe around base of each cake. Use fingertip to blend icing into any gaps where cakes join the boards (page 94). Dry cakes overnight.

6 To make pleated strips: Roll 200g (6½ ounces) of the remaining icing at a time on cornfloured surface into two strips 3mm (⅛-inch) thick. Using the perspex measure and pizza cutter, cut strips of icing 3.7cm wide and 30cm (12 inches) long (see step 1, page 57).

7 Position 5 of the wooden skewers parallel to the edge of the bench, about 1cm (½ inch) apart. Lift icing strips over the top of the skewers (see step 2, page 57). Place 5 remaining skewers on top of the icing, in between the first skewers (see step 3, page 57). Gently push the skewers closer together to pleat the icing (see step 4, page 57). Carefully remove skewers, and reposition them under and on top of the next section of the icing strip (see step 5, page 57). Continue until the strips are pleated.

8 Use paint brush to brush bottom 3cm (1¼-inch) of cake sparingly with water. Carefully lift pleated strip and secure into position around cake (see step 6, page 57); cutting strip to fit cake. Continue this process all around the base of the cake, joining, trimming and slightly overlapping the ends of the strips. Repeat with remaining strips on remaining cake tiers. Stand cake overnight until pleats dry.

9 Measure around base of cake; trim ribbon to fit around cake, securing to pleats with tiny dots of royal icing. Make small bows (page 106) to cover joins in ribbon; secure bows with royal icing. Secure perspex initials to cake with a little royal icing.

Continues overleaf

Continues from previous page

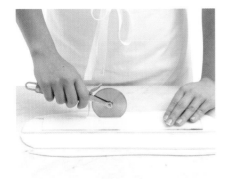

Step 1 Roll the ready-made icing into a long thin strip. Use the perspex measure and pizza cutter to cut 2 strips to make the pleats.

Step 2 Position 5 thick wooden skewers on the bench top, about 1cm apart. Carefully lift the strips of icing over the top of the skewers.

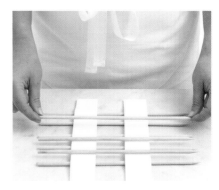

Step 3 Position another 5 skewers on top of the icing; place them between the skewers that are positioned underneath the icing.

Step 4 Using cornfloured fingers, gently push the skewers on top of and underneath the icing together to make a pleat in the icing.

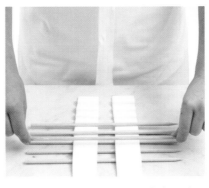

Step 5 Remove the skewers gently from the icing; reposition the skewers as close as possible to the last pleat and continue to pleat the strip.

Step 6 Lift pleated strip into position around the cake. Overlap the next pleated strip to make neat joins. Dry the pleats overnight.

tips It's important to allow time for the icing on the assembled cakes to dry before positioning the strips; use the thick wooden skewers to gently press the pleats into position on the dampened icing.

The pleated strips need to be slightly firm, but still pliable enough to wrap around the cakes without cracking or breaking. You may need to join 2 strips for the larger cakes; overlap the next pleated strip to make neat joins. While we used perspex initials on this cake, there are many different types, shapes and sizes available.

21st celebration cake

EQUIPMENT

30cm (12-inch) round wooden cake board (page 90)

15cm (6-inch) round wooden cake board (page 90)

smoothing tools

4 wooden cake skewers

2 paper piping bags (page 103)

number 1 and 2 cutters

2 x 10cm (4-inch) pieces 18-gauge floral wire

artist's fine paint brush

pasta machine (see tips, page 60)

1cm (½-inch) plain piping tube

CAKE

deep 20cm (8-inch) round cake of choice (page 107)

deep 15cm (6-inch) round cake of choice (page 107)

DECORATIONS

1.5kg (3 pounds) ready-made white icing

cornflour (cornstarch)

pale blue, rose pink, yellow and orange food colourings

1 quantity royal icing (page 102)

3 teaspoons tylose powder

1 Trim cakes (page 91). Secure large cake to largest board; secure small cake to remaining board. Prepare cakes for covering with ready-made icing (page 91).

2 Knead 1kg (2 pounds) of the ready-made icing on surface dusted with a little cornflour until icing loses its stickiness. Tint with blue colouring. Roll 400g (12½ ounces) of the blue icing on cornfloured surface until large enough to cover small cake. Using rolling pin, lift icing onto cake; smooth with hands then smoothing tools. Trim icing neatly around base. Use remaining icing to cover large cake in the same way. Dry cakes overnight. Reserve icing scraps, enclose in plastic wrap.

3 Push 3 trimmed skewers into centre of large cake to support top tier. Secure small cake on top of large cake (page 94).

4 Tint royal icing blue to match cakes. Half-fill piping bag with royal icing; pipe around base of each cake. Use fingertip to blend icing into any gaps where cakes join the boards (page 94). Dry overnight. Cover the surface of the remaining royal icing with plastic wrap to prevent it drying out.

5 Knead reserved blue icing scraps with three-quarters of the remaining white icing on cornfloured surface; tint icing to a darker blue colour.

6 Knead 1 teaspoon of the tylose powder into half of the dark blue icing; roll out into a 6mm (¼-inch) thickness on surface dusted with cornflour. Use cutters to cut out numbers (see step 1, page 60). Dip one end of both pieces of wire about 2cm (¾-inch) into water. Push wet end of wires into the bases of both numbers (see step 2, page 60). Place numbers on baking-paper-covered tray to dry overnight or until firm.

7 Roll remaining dark blue icing into 6mm-thick rope shapes (see step 3, page 60). Brush lightly around base of cakes with a little water, gently position icing ropes around cakes. Carefully join ends.

8 Divide remaining white icing into 4 portions. Tint with pink, yellow and orange colourings. Leave remaining portion white. Cover with plastic wrap.

9 To make strips: Knead ½ teaspoon tylose into one portion of icing. Roll out on cornfloured surface into a 3mm (⅛-inch) thickness; roll through a pasta machine until 2mm (1⁄16-inch) thick (see step 4, page 60). Cut 1cm x 10cm (½-inch x 4-inch) strips from icing. Coil strips around remaining skewer (see step 5, page 60); carefully remove skewer. Use the tip of piping tube to cut dots from leftover scraps of icing (see step 6, page 60). Stand strips and dots on baking-paper-lined tray for 30 minutes or until barely firm. Repeat with remaining coloured icings.

10 Push wired numbers into cake. Three-quarters fill piping bag with royal icing. Decorate cake with 'confetti' and 'ribbons', securing to the cake with tiny dots of royal icing.

Continues overleaf

Step 1 Knead a teaspoon of tylose powder into one-third of the icing. Roll icing out on cornfloured surface to cut out numbers.

Step 2 Dip ends of both wires into water about 2cm. Push wet ends of wire about half-way into the number shapes. Dry numbers overnight.

Step 3 Roll icing into rope shape long enough to wrap around cakes. Brush a little water around cake bases and carefully position icing ropes.

Step 4 To make decorations, feed the icing through a pasta machine set on the thickest setting; or if you prefer, roll out icing until about 2mm thick.

Step 5 Coil strips of icing around a thick wooden skewer, place on baking-paper-lined tray to dry for about 3 hours or overnight.

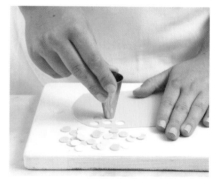

Step 6 Use tip of piping tube to cut out dots from different coloured icings. Dry for 3 hours or overnight on a baking-paper-lined tray.

tips There are no special cake decorating skills required for this celebratory cake. While the decorations can be made by rolling the icing out thinly to 2mm, rolling the icing through a pasta machine gives great results. The numbers should be positioned in the cake on the day of serving.

Continues from previous page

Broderie anglaise lace cake

EQUIPMENT

25cm (10-inch) square wooden cake board (page 90)

15cm (6-inch) square wooden cake board (page 90)

smoothing tools

4 wooden cake skewers

artist's medium paint brush

tape measure & plastic ruler

scalloped-edge frill cutter

set of eyelet cutters

1.5cm & 2cm (¾ inch) flower cutters

fine pearl-headed pin

small piping bag

small (number 2) plain piping tube

tweezers

22cm (8¾-inch) 20-gauge floral wire

CAKE

deep 20cm (8-inch) square cake of choice (page 107)

deep 15cm (6-inch) square cake of choice (page 107)

DECORATIONS

1.6kg (3¼ pounds) ready-made white icing

cornflour (cornstarch)

pink food colouring

1 quantity royal icing (page 102)

silver cachous

1 Trim cakes (page 91). Secure 20cm cake to largest board; secure small cake to remaining board. Prepare cakes for covering with ready-made icing (page 91).

2 Knead ready-made icing on surface dusted with a little cornflour until icing loses its stickiness. Roll 400g (12½ ounces) of icing on cornfloured surface until large enough to cover small cake. Using rolling pin, lift icing onto cake; smooth with hands then smoothing tools. Trim icing neatly around base of cake.

3 Use 550g (1 pound) of the icing to cover large cake in the same way. Dry cakes overnight.

4 Push trimmed skewers into centre of large cake to support the top tier (page 94). Secure small cake to large cake. Dry cakes overnight.

5 Use paint brush to lightly brush water around sides of cakes to cover where the pink bands of icing will be positioned.

6 Tint remaining icing pink, reserve one-third of the icing in plastic wrap.

7 Measure around large cake. Roll icing into a strip long enough to wrap around cake and wide enough to almost cover sides of cake. Using a ruler and knife, or pizza cutter, cut icing into a neat strip, almost as wide as the side of the cake. Lift into position around cake. Repeat with small cake.

8 Gently press frill cutter, at an angle, into top of pink icing to scallop edge; remove excess icing (see step 1). Using eyelet and flower cutters, and picture as a guide, cut out or mark random shapes on the cakes. Use the pin to remove some of the cut pieces (see step 2).

9 Tint royal icing pink. Fit piping bag with tube. Half-fill bag with icing; pipe around scallop edges and some of the cut outs (see step 3).

10 Using tweezers, secure cachous to cakes with a little royal icing. Stand cake overnight to dry.

11 Re-roll scraps of pink icing, cut out several flower shapes; insert pieces of floral wire into shapes, stand on baking-paper-covered tray to dry overnight. Position wired flowers on day of serving.

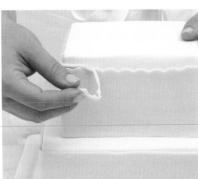

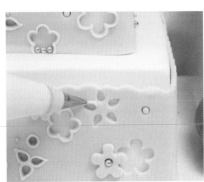

Step 1 Carefully press scalloped-edged frill cutter against the top edge of the icing strip on both cakes; gently remove excess icing.

Step 2 Using a fine pin, remove some cut-out pieces of icing; leave some intact. Stick some flower cut-outs to the cake with royal icing.

Step 3 Tint royal icing pale pink. Half-fill the piping bag with icing, and pipe around the scalloped edges and some of the cut-outs.

Step 1 As soon as the cake has been covered with icing, gently press the cutter into the icing starting from the bottom of the cake.

Step 2 Use the perspex measure and a sharp knife to trim the ribbon into a 2.5cm width. Don't cut through the icing underneath.

Step 3 Pipe a line about 5cm long; position pearls with tweezers on icing before it sets. Repeat with icing and pearls around the cake.

Mint & pink pearl cake

EQUIPMENT

30cm (12-inch) round wooden cake board (page 90)

15cm (6-inch) round wooden cake board (page 90)

smoothing tools

3cm x 3.5cm (1¼-inch x 1½-inch) scalloped cutter

3 wooden skewers

2 paper piping bags (page 103)

tape measure

artist's fine paint brush

2.5cm (1-inch) perspex measure

tweezers

CAKE

deep 20cm (8-inch) round cake of choice (page 107)

deep 15cm (6-inch) round cake of choice (page 107)

DECORATIONS

1kg (2 pounds) ready-made white icing

cornflour (cornstarch)

rose pink and kelly green food colourings

1 quantity royal icing (page 102)

113g (3½-ounce) packet pearlized blush sugar pearls

1 Trim cakes (page 91). Secure large cake to largest board; secure small cake to remaining board. Prepare cakes for covering with ready-made icing (page 91).

2 Knead ready-made icing on surface dusted with a little cornflour until icing loses its stickiness. Tint 100g (3 ounces) of the icing pink, enclose in plastic wrap. Tint the remaining icing green.

3 Roll 400g (12½ ounces) of green icing on cornfloured surface until large enough to cover small cake. Using rolling pin, lift icing onto cake; smooth with hands then smoothing tools. Trim icing neatly around base of cake. Use remaining green icing plus any scraps to cover large cake in the same way as the small cake.

4 Carefully press scallop cutter around side and over the top edge of large cake while the icing is still soft (see step 1). Dry cakes overnight.

5 Push trimmed skewers into centre of large cake to support top tier (page 94). Secure small cake to large cake.

6 Colour half the royal icing the same green as the cakes. Three-quarters fill a piping bag with icing. Pipe green icing around base of each cake. Use fingertip to blend icing into any gaps where cakes join the boards (page 94). Dry cakes overnight.

7 Measure around base of top tier. Roll pink icing on cornfloured surface into a 2mm (¹⁄₁₆-inch) thickness, and long enough to wrap around cake. Cut a straight edge down one long side. Brush bottom 2cm (¾-inch) of small cake sparingly with water; secure icing strip around base, trim ends neatly. Use perspex measure and a small sharp knife to trim strip into a 2.5cm-wide ribbon; don't cut into icing underneath (see step 2).

8 Re-roll pink icing scraps into a 3mm (⅛-inch) thickness. Using scallop cutter, cut a scallop from the icing; secure to side of small cake with a little water.

9 Tint remaining royal icing pale pink. Half-fill piping bag with icing; pipe decorations onto cake. Pipe a 5cm (2-inch) line of pink icing around base of small cake, position pearls on icing before it sets (see step 3). Repeat all around cake.

tips Mark the pattern on the icing before it sets — do it carefully and slowly and you'll be pleased with the outcome. The 'pearlized blush sugar pearls' are small edible pearls, and are available from cake decorating suppliers. The cutter we used came from a kit of patchwork cutters.

Christmas snowflakes

EQUIPMENT

25cm (10-inch) round wooden cake board (page 90)

smoothing tools

set of 3 snowflake plunger cutters (small, medium, large)

artist's fine paint brush

paper piping bag (page 103)

CAKE

deep 20cm (8-inch) round cake of choice (page 107)

DECORATIONS

750g (1½ pounds) ready-made white icing

cornflour (cornstarch)

cornflower blue food colouring

1 teaspoon tylose powder

1 egg white, lightly beaten

½ cup (110g) white sanding sugar

1 quantity royal icing (page 102)

180g (5½ ounces) small persian confetti

1 Trim cake (page 91). Secure cake to board. Prepare for covering with ready-made icing (page 91).

2 Knead ready-made icing on surface dusted with a little cornflour until icing loses its stickiness. Tint three-quarters of the icing blue with colouring.

3 Roll out blue icing on cornfloured surface into a 3mm (⅛-inch) thickness. Using rolling pin, lift icing over cake; smooth with hands then smoothing tools. Trim icing neatly around base of cake.

4 Knead remaining white ready-made icing with tylose powder on surface dusted with cornflour until smooth. Roll out on surface dusted with cornflour into a 3mm (⅛-inch) thickness. Use cutters to cut out different-sized snowflakes. Place snowflakes on baking-paper-lined tray to dry overnight.

5 Brush a very thin layer of egg white onto tips and around the centres of snowflake shapes (see step 1); sprinkle sanding sugar over egg white. Stand the snowflakes for about 1 hour or until dry (see step 2).

6 Meanwhile, three-quarters fill piping bag with royal icing. Pipe a line of icing all the way around base of cake. Position persian confetti on icing before it dries.

7 Secure snowflakes to cake with royal icing (see step 3); leave to dry for about 1 hour.

tips The sanding sugar gives the snowflakes a lovely texture, however, if you can't find it, don't worry, the snowflakes look divine without it. Snowflakes can be made months ahead; store them in an airtight container at room temperature. Persian confetti is sometimes sold as 'snowfall'. A fine dusting of sifted icing sugar added at the last minute adds to the snowy look.

Step 1 Using a fine artist's paint brush, brush a very thin layer of egg white onto the tips and around the centres of all the snowflakes.

Step 2 Sprinkle the centres and tips of the snowflakes with the sanding sugar; stand the snowflakes for about 1 hour or until dry.

Step 3 Pipe royal icing on the back of a snowflake, position on cake; hold large snowflakes for about 5 seconds or until they grip the cake.

Step 1 Using the fine wooden skewer, mark grooves of random lengths around the sides of all the cakes. Do this before the icing sets.

Step 2 Press small amounts of icing into mould. Scrape away excess icing. Remove flowers from mould; dry overnight.

Step 3 Pipe vertical lines of royal icing into the grooves using white and three shades of pink icing. Leave some grooves without icing.

Pink on white flower cake

EQUIPMENT

35cm (14-inch) round wooden cake board (page 90)

20cm (8-inch) round wooden cake board (page 90)

15cm (6-inch) round wooden cake board (page 90)

smoothing tools

fine long wooden skewer

6 wooden cake skewers

silicone flower mould

small metal spatula

4 small piping bags

small (number 2) plain piping tube

CAKE

deep 25cm (10-inch) round cake of choice (page 107)

deep 20cm (8-inch) round cake of choice (page 107)

deep 15cm (6-inch) round cake of choice (page 107)

DECORATIONS

2kg (4 pounds) ready-made white icing

cornflour (cornstarch)

tylose powder

rose pink food colouring

1 quantity royal icing (page 102)

1   Knead ready-made icing on surface dusted with a little cornflour until icing loses its stickiness. Reserve 200g (6½ ounces) of icing for flowers.

2   Trim cakes (page 91). Secure 25cm cake to largest board; secure remaining cakes to same-sized boards. Prepare cakes for covering with ready-made icing (page 91).

3   Roll 400g (12½ ounces) of the icing on surface dusted with cornflour until large enough to cover small cake. Using rolling pin, lift icing onto cake; smooth with hands then smoothing tools. Trim icing neatly around base of cake.

4   Use 600g (1¼ pounds) of the icing to cover medium cake in the same way as small cake. Use remaining icing to cover large cake. Reserve icing scraps.

5   Use the fine wooden skewer to mark the icing in random lengths all around cakes before the icing sets (see step 1). Dry cakes overnight.

6   Push 3 trimmed skewers into centres of large and medium cakes to support top tiers (page 94). Assemble cakes, securing each tier to the tier below.

7   Knead ½ teaspoon tylose powder into reserved icing and scraps. Divide icing into four portions; colour three portions different shades of pink. Leave remaining portion white. Press small amounts of each coloured icing into flower moulds; using spatula, scrape excess icing from backs of flowers so the shapes are flush with the mould. Bend mould gently to release flowers (see step 2). Place the flowers, top-side up, on baking-paper-lined tray to dry overnight.

8   Fit piping bag with tube. Half-fill bag with royal icing; pipe a line of small teardrops around base of each cake. Pipe white vertical lines in some of the grooves on the cakes (see step 3). Wash and dry piping tube; place in a clean piping bag.

9   Mix leftover icing in piping bag with remaining royal icing; divide between three small bowls. Colour each batch a different shade of pink; cover surface with plastic wrap to keep airtight. Working with one colour at a time, pipe vertical lines in some of the grooves on the cakes. Repeat with remaining icings leaving some grooves plain. Wash and dry piping tube after each colour.

10   Using a few flowers at a time, pipe a little royal icing onto back of flowers; secure over cake in a random pattern.

tips Silicone moulds come in myriad shapes and sizes. The mould we used gave us three different-sized flowers.

Divine white silk rose cake

EQUIPMENT

30cm (12-inch) round wooden cake board (page 90)

15cm (6-inch) round wooden cake board (page 90)

smoothing tools

number 3 strip cutter 7mm (¼-inch) wide

3 wooden cake skewers

2 paper piping bags (page 103)

white florist's tape

CAKE

deep 20cm (8-inch) round cake of choice (page 107)

2 x deep 15cm (6-inch) round cakes of choice (page 107)

jam or ganache of choice (page 92)

DECORATIONS

1kg (2 pounds) ready-made white icing

cornflour (cornstarch)

green food colouring

1 quantity royal icing (page 102)

1m (1 yard) wide ribbon

1m (1 yard) narrow ribbon

white silk cabbage rose or fresh organic flowers

1 Trim cakes (page 91). Secure large cake to largest board. Secure one 15cm cake to same-sized cake board; top with remaining 15cm cake, joining with a little jam or ganache. Prepare cakes for covering with ready-made icing (pages 91).

2 Knead ready-made icing on surface dusted with a little cornflour until icing loses its stickiness. Tint half the icing pale green.

3 Roll green icing on cornfloured surface until large enough to cover 20cm cake. Using rolling pin, lift icing onto cake; smooth with hands then smoothing tools. Trim icing neatly around base.

4 Use white icing to cover 15cm cake in the same way. While icing is still soft, use strip cutter to mark grooves into the icing on the top tier (see step 1). Stand cakes overnight to dry.

5 Push trimmed skewers into centre of large cake to support the top tier. Secure small cake on top of large cake (page 94).

6 Tint half the royal icing green to match the bottom tier. Three-quarters fill a piping bag with icing; pipe around base of cake. Use fingertip to blend icing into any gaps where cake joins the board (page 94). Repeat process using white royal icing for top tier. Stand cakes overnight to dry.

7 Wrap ribbons around base of bottom cake; cut to fit. Secure ends with a little white royal icing (see step 2).

8 Trim silk flower to fit top of cake (see step 3). Wrap stem in white florist's tape. Gently prise open flower petals; lay flower on top of cake.

tips The strip cutter, used for marking the icing on the top tier of this cake, is very useful if the icing is not quite perfect. It's important to mark the grooves on the icing before it begins to develop a crust and becomes firm. Position the flower on the day of serving. This cake is topped with a fabulous silk cabbage rose; if you prefer, buy fresh organic flowers to decorate the cake on the day of serving.

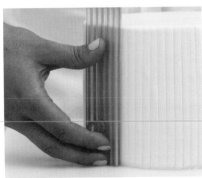

Step 1 Using the strip cutter, gently, but evenly, press it onto the soft icing before the icing begins to dry and develops a crust.

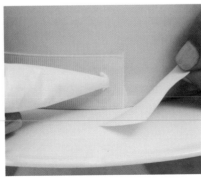

Step 2 Measure around the base of the bottom tier; cut ribbons to fit. Position and secure ribbons to cake with tiny dabs of royal icing.

Step 3 Trim the stem, leaves and buds of the silk rose to fit the cake; tape stems with florist's tape. Gently prise open the flower petals.

Wedding cake wonder

EQUIPMENT

drill

12mm (½ inch) drill bit with centring tip
(see tips, page 73)

35cm (14-inch) round wooden cake board (page 90)

30cm (12-inch) round wooden cake board (page 90)

25cm (10-inch) round wooden cake board (page 90)

20cm (8-inch) round wooden cake board (page 90)

15cm (6-inch) round wooden cake board (page 90)

9cm x 20cm (3¾-inch x 8-inch) diameter
styrofoam disc

9cm x 15cm (3¾-inch x 6-inch) diameter
styrofoam disc

9cm x 10cm (3¾-inch x 4-inch) diameter
styrofoam disc

craft glue (or glue gun)

12mm x 60cm (½-inch x 24-inch) wooden dowel

smoothing tools

pastry brush

plastic ruler

pizza cutter

pencil

fine pearl-headed pins

small piping bag

small (number 2) plain piping tube

7 wooden cake skewers

CAKE

deep 25cm (10-inch) round cake of choice (page 107)

shallow 25cm (10-inch) round cake of choice (page 107)

deep 20cm (8-inch) round cake of choice (page 107)

shallow 20cm (8-inch) round cake of choice (page 107)

deep 15cm (6-inch) round cake of choice (page 107)

shallow 15cm (6-inch) round cake of choice (page 107)

ganache or jam of choice (pages 92, 99)

DECORATIONS

2.5kg (5 pounds) ready-made ivory icing

cornflour (cornstarch)

1 quantity sugar syrup (page 99)

1 quantity royal icing (page 102)

rose pink food colouring

fresh large organic flowers

1 Knead 500g (1 pound) ready-made icing on surface dusted with a little cornflour until icing loses its stickiness. Brush 35cm board with sugar syrup. Roll icing large enough to cover board (page 90). Using rolling pin, lift icing onto board; smooth with hands then smoothing tools. Trim icing neatly around base; use cornfloured fingertip to smooth edge. Stand overnight to dry.

2 Mark the centre of each cake board and styrofoam disc. Except for the 30cm wooden board, drill a 12mm hole through the centre of each disc and each board. Glue the 35cm board on top of the 30cm board (this gives clearance under the board so you can pick it up off the bench). Squeeze glue into hole in the 35cm board; position dowel in the hole (see step 1, page 75). Stand until dry.

3 Trim cakes (page 91). Secure deep 25cm cake to largest board. Secure remaining deep cakes to same-sized boards. Position shallow cakes on top of same-sized deep cakes; secure with jam or ganache. Prepare cakes for covering with ready-made icing (page 91).

4 Knead icing on surface dusted with a little cornflour until icing loses its stickiness. Roll 375g (12 ounces) of icing on cornfloured surface until large enough to cover small cake. Using rolling pin, lift icing onto cake; smooth with hands then smoothing tools. Trim icing neatly around base.

5 Use 625g (1¼ pounds) of icing to cover medium cake and use 750g (1½ pounds) of icing to cover large cake in the same way as small cake. Dry cakes overnight.

6 Using one styrofoam disc at a time, brush sugar syrup sparingly around sides of discs. Roll 80g (2½ ounces) icing on cornfloured surface until long enough to wrap around side of smallest disc; using ruler and pizza cutter, trim to fit. Cover side of styrofoam (see step 2, page 75); reserve scraps. Trim away any excess icing on top and bottom of disc (see step 3, page 75). Knead scraps and remaining icing together; cover sides of remaining discs in the same way.

7 Using picture as a guide, draw 'stitch' pattern onto a strip of baking paper large enough to wrap around large cake (see step 4, page 75); attach to cake, marked-side out, using pins. Using a fine pin, mark pattern onto each cake (see step 5, page 75), reducing the length of the paper to fit around the middle cake, then the small cake.

8 Tint royal icing pale pink. Fit piping bag with tube. Three-quarters fill bag with royal icing; pipe pattern onto cakes using pin marks as a guide (see step 6, page 75); leave to dry for at least 1 hour.

9 To assemble the cake: Position the largest styrofoam disc onto the dowel, secure to board with a little royal icing (see step 7, page 75). Next, firmly push the large cake down over the dowel (see step 8, page 75); secure to the disc below with royal icing. Push 3 trimmed skewers into top of large cake (page 94). Top with the medium disc then medium cake in the same way; push 3 trimmed skewers into medium cake. Top with the small disc then small cake.

10 Use remaining wooden skewer to pierce holes into side of styrofoam discs. Push flower stems into holes (see step 9, page 75) to fill the gaps between the cakes with flowers. Lay more flowers on top of cake. Position flowers on the day of serving.

tips The drill bit should be suitable for drilling wood. Discuss the type of flowers to be used with a florist to make sure they'll stay fresh. Use artificial flowers, if you prefer. The styrofoam discs are used to support the flowers between each cake tier.

73

Continues overleaf

Continues from previous page

Step 1 Drill 1cm holes in all the discs and boards except for the 30cm wooden board. Use glue to secure the dowel into position.

Step 2 Lightly brush the sides of the discs with sugar syrup. Cut strips of icing long and wide enough to wrap around sides of discs.

Step 3 Use a sharp knife to cut away any excess icing from the top and bottom of each disc. Be careful not to cut into the disc.

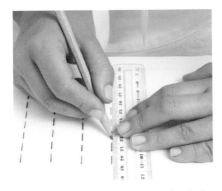

Step 4 Measure around cake using a band of baking paper; using pencil and ruler, draw 'stitch' markings of varying lengths onto the paper.

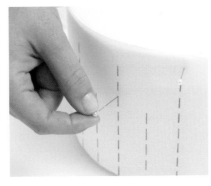

Step 5 Secure the band of baking paper (marked-side outwards) around the cake with fine pins. Mark the pattern onto the cake with pins.

Step 6 Remove baking paper. Fit piping bag with tube and, following the pin markings, pipe the pattern onto the cakes. Leave to dry.

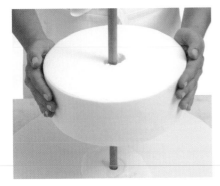

Step 7 Position the largest disc on the dowel; secure to board with royal icing. Spread more royal icing on top of the disc.

Step 8 Push the large cake onto the dowel to meet the disc. Push the trimmed skewers into the cake to support the next disc.

Step 9 Push a wooden skewer into the disc; wriggle it around to make holes large enough to hold the flower stems firmly in position.

A posy of daisies

EQUIPMENT

2.5cm (1-inch) flower cutter

1.5cm (¾-inch) flower cutter

vinyl mat

flower mat

small ball tool

metal skewer

10cm (4-inch) styrofoam ball

1cm x 20cm (½-inch x 8-inch) wooden dowel

craft glue

small styrofoam block

30cm (12-inch) round wooden cake board (page 90)

15cm (6-inch) round wooden cake board (page 90)

smoothing tools

3 wooden cake skewers

paper piping bag (page 103)

pastry brush

CAKE

deep 20cm (8-inch) round cake of choice (page 107)

deep 15cm (6-inch) round cake of choice (page 107)

1 quantity sugar syrup (page 99)

DECORATIONS

150g (4½ ounces) modelling paste

cornflour (cornstarch)

1m (1 yard) narrow white ribbon

1kg (2 pounds) ready-made white icing

lemon yellow food colouring

1 quantity royal icing (page 102)

1 Knead modelling paste on surface dusted with a little cornflour until paste loses its stickiness. Roll paste out on cornfloured surface into a 1mm (1/32-inch) thickness. Using both cutters, cut out 5 flowers of each size at a time. Cover paste with vinyl mat to prevent it drying out.

2 Place 5 flowers on the flower mat; using the ball tool, press into the centre of each flower, in a circular motion, until the flower has thinned out and curled into a cup shape (see step 1, page 79). Place the flowers on a fine wire rack or a baking-paper-lined tray to dry. Repeat process until all the paste is used.

3 Push the metal skewer halfway into the styrofoam ball and wriggle it around to create a hole large enough to push the dowel into (see step 2, page 79). Place a little glue around one end of the dowel, push dowel into hole in the ball. Stand 1 hour to dry. Spread a little glue along the back of the ribbon. Starting at the top of the dowel, wrap ribbon around the dowel. (see step 3, page 79) Allow to dry; stand ball upright in the styrofoam block to support it.

4 Trim cakes (page 91). Secure large cake to largest board; secure small cake to remaining board. Prepare cakes for covering with ready-made icing (page 91).

5 Knead ready-made icing on surface dusted with a little cornflour until icing loses its stickiness. Tint icing pale yellow.

6 Roll 300g (9½ ounces) of the icing on cornfloured surface until large enough to cover small cake. Using rolling pin, lift icing onto cake; smooth with hands then smoothing tools. Trim icing neatly around base.

7 Using 500g (1 pound) of the icing, cover large cake in the same way. Dry cakes overnight.

8 Push trimmed skewers into centre of large cake to support the top tier (page 94). Secure small cake to large cake (page 94).

9 Tint royal icing yellow to match cakes. Three-quarters fill piping bag with royal icing; pipe around base of each cake. Use fingertip to blend icing into any gaps where cakes join the boards (page 94). Dry overnight.

10 Pipe yellow centres into each of the flowers with royal icing (see step 4, page 79); stand flowers 3 hours or overnight to dry.

11 Brush styrofoam ball lightly with sugar syrup. Roll out remaining yellow icing until large enough to cover the ball. Using rolling pin, lift icing onto ball; smooth with hands (see step 5, page 79) then smoothing tools. Trim icing neatly around base of the ball.

12 Push dowel through the centre of the top cake until it reaches the board below. Using small and large flowers, pipe a dot of royal icing onto the back of a flower, position on the ball (see step 6, page 79). Continue positioning flowers to cover the ball.

13 Using picture as a guide, use flowers to decorate both cakes. Leave completed cake to dry overnight.

Continues overleaf

Continues from previous page

Step 1 Using the flower mat and the ball tool, shape flowers until a cup shape has formed and the petals become thinner.

Step 2 Using the large metal skewer, pierce the styrofoam ball. Wriggle it around to make a hole large enough for the dowel to fit snuggly.

Step 3 Glue dowel into ball; stand 1 hour to dry. Glue ribbon to dowel; wind it around dowel to the bottom, without completely covering.

Step 4 Three-quarters fill a piping bag with yellow royal icing. Pipe dots in all the flower centres; leave flowers to dry overnight.

Step 5 Brush styrofoam ball lightly with sugar syrup. Gently mould icing over ball, making it as neat as possible. Trim away excess icing.

Step 6 Pipe a dab of royal icing onto back of a flower, position on styrofoam ball. Continue using large and small flowers to cover ball.

tips Modelling paste is also sold as 'petal paste', 'flower moulding paste' and 'gum paste'.

There are no special piping skills required for this cake, but covering the ball can be a little tricky. Drape the rolled ready-made icing over the ball – it will hang with loose folds. Gently, without stretching, ease the folds out of the icing as you press the icing onto and around the ball. Trim off excess icing at the base of the ball. There should be no creases in the icing if done correctly.

Wedding cake pops

EQUIPMENT

20cm x 30cm (8-inch x 12-inch) rectangular cake pan

20cm (8-inch) styrofoam block

2.5cm (1-inch) round cutter

3cm (1¼-inch) round cutter

3.5cm (1½-inch) round cutter

5cm (2-inch) round cutter

18 long thin toothpicks

18 x 30cm (12-inch) cake pop sticks

paper piping bag (page 103)

tweezers

metal skewer

ruler

CAKE

5 cups firmly packed butter cake crumbs

½ quantity butter cream (page 100)

DECORATIONS

3 x 375g (12-ounce) packets white chocolate Melts

golden yellow and black food colourings

1 quantity royal icing (page 102)

1 packet 2mm (1/16-inch) white sugar pearls

9 white sugar flowers

50g (1½ ounces) ready-made white icing

cornflour (cornstarch)

4m (4 yards) narrow ribbon

1 Grease and line rectangular pan with baking paper. Combine cake crumbs and butter cream in medium bowl. Press mixture evenly into pan; cover, freeze 1 hour or refrigerate overnight until firm.

2 Stir two-thirds of the chocolate in medium heatproof bowl over medium saucepan of simmering water until smooth (don't let water touch base of bowl, page 104). Transfer to tall narrow heatproof glass or jug.

3 Meanwhile, use a sharp pointed knife to make 18 small holes, about 5cm (2 inches) apart, in styrofoam.

4 To make all cake pops: For the hats, use 3cm cutter to cut 18 rounds from the cake crumb mixture. For the wedding cakes, cut 9 x 2.5cm rounds, 9 x 3.5cm rounds and 9 x 5cm rounds (see step 1, page 83).

5 To make wedding cake pops: Dip the end of a toothpick into melted white chocolate; push about halfway into the middle of a 2.5cm round. Repeat with remaining toothpicks and remaining 2.5cm and 3.5cm rounds. Freeze cakes about 5 minutes.

6 Dip the end of a cake pop stick into white chocolate; push stick all the way through 5cm round, extending about 4.5cm past the top of the cake (see step 2, page 83). Repeat with remaining cake pop sticks and remaining 5cm rounds. Freeze cakes about 5 minutes.

7 Dip wedding cake rounds in melted chocolate to coat; rock back and forth, don't twist or cakes will break (re-melt chocolate as necessary). Stand upright in styrofoam, refrigerate until set.

8 To assemble wedding cakes; scrape away any excess visible chocolate from the toothpicks or cake pop sticks to prevent damaging any of the tiers (see step 3, page 83). Remove 3.5cm rounds from toothpicks, carefully push onto cake pop sticks on top of the 5cm rounds. Repeat with 2.5cm rounds (see step 4, page 83). Use a little melted white chocolate to join tiers together.

9 Use a tiny bit of yellow colouring to tint the royal icing the same colour as the chocolate on the wedding cakes (see tips, page 83). Half-fill paper piping bag with icing, use to fill any gaps between tiers of cakes; smooth icing with fingertip.

10 Pipe tiny dots around base of 2.5cm and 3.5cm tiers; using tweezers, position sugar pearls in wet icing. Repeat all the way around cakes. Secure flowers to cakes with a little royal icing.

11 To make top hats: Melt remaining chocolate; use black colouring to tint chocolate grey. Transfer chocolate to tall narrow heatproof glass or jug. Dip end of cake pop stick into chocolate; push stick through 2 x 3cm rounds (see step 5, page 83) about halfway into the top round. Join rounds with a little melted chocolate; freeze cakes about 5 minutes. Dip hats in melted grey chocolate to coat (re-melt chocolate, if necessary); stand upright in styrofoam, refrigerate until set.

12 To make brims for hats: re-melt grey chocolate as necessary, spread onto a sheet of baking paper about 2mm (1/16-inch) thick. Stand about 10 minutes or until almost set.

13 Use 5cm-round cutter to cut 9 rounds from chocolate. Use a metal skewer to pierce a hole through the centre of the rounds (heat skewer if the chocolate has become too hard); thread onto cake pop sticks (see step 6, page 83). Secure with chocolate. Return cake pop sticks to styrofoam, refrigerate until set.

14 Roll ready-made icing on surface dusted with a little cornflour until icing loses its stickiness. Roll icing on surface dusted with cornflour until 2mm thick. Cut icing into 9 strips, measuring 1cm x 8cm (1/2-inch x 3 1/4-inches) (they should be long enough to wrap around the hat). Secure bands to hats with a little royal icing.

15 Tie small bows (page 106) around cake pop sticks.

Continues overleaf

Step 1 The cake crumb mixture must be frozen or very firm before cutting out rounds for the wedding cake and top hat cake pops.

Step 2 Dip ends of the cake pop sticks into chocolate; push sticks through large rounds, extending about 4.5cm past top of cake.

Step 3 Dip all the tiers for the wedding cake in melted chocolate. Let excess chocolate drip off, then level under each tier with a knife.

Step 4 Push the medium and small tiers onto the extended cake pop stick; secure the tiers together with a little melted chocolate.

Step 5 Push two of the cake rounds for the top hats onto a cake pop stick to form the hats. Join rounds with a little melted chocolate.

Step 6 Push a round of chocolate onto cake pop stick to make the brim of the hat. Secure brim to hat with a little melted chocolate.

tips Cut out cake rounds as close as possible. Squash and press remaining cake mixture together, freeze and cut out more shapes, if necessary. Because the royal icing is very white, and the white chocolate is a creamy colour, it is necessary to tint the icing with a tiny bit of yellow food colouring to give it a creamy colour so it blends with the white chocolate. Re-melt the chocolate as necessary (page 104).

Store the wedding cake pops at a cool room temperature, standing up in styrofoam, covered, to protect them from dust. Or, store them flat in airtight containers. The cake pops are fiddly to make, but are well worth the effort. We used little sugar roses, bought from the supermarket, to decorate the wedding cakes.

Kitchen tea biscuits

MAKES 20

EQUIPMENT

oven trays

6cm x 9cm (2½-inch x 3¾-inch) teacup cutter

6.5cm x 7.5cm (2¾-inch x 3-inch) teapot cutter

pastry brush

small piping bag

small (number 2) plain piping tube

1.4cm (¾-inch) blossom cutter

2.5cm (1-inch) blossom cutter

tweezers

BISCUITS

125g (4 ounces) butter

2 eggs

1 teaspoon vanilla extract

⅔ cup (150g) caster (superfine) sugar

1⅓ cups (200g) self-raising flour

1 cup (150g) plain (all-purpose) flour

DECORATIONS

500g (1 pound) ready-made white icing

cornflour (cornstarch)

mauve, rose pink, sky blue, leaf green and golden yellow food colourings

1 egg white, beaten lightly

1 quantity royal icing (page 102)

2 teaspoons pearlized blush sugar pearls

1 Have butter and eggs at room temperature for biscuits.

2 To make biscuits: Beat butter, extract and sugar in small bowl with electric mixer until combined. Beat in eggs, one at a time; beat only until combined. (Do not overbeat; mixture will curdle at this stage, but will come together later.) Transfer mixture to large bowl. Stir in sifted flours in two batches; mix to a soft dough. Knead dough on floured surface until smooth; cover, refrigerate 30 minutes.

3 Preheat oven to 180°C/350°F. Grease and line oven trays with baking paper.

4 Roll dough between sheets of baking paper until 5mm (¼-inch) thick. Using teacup and teapot cutters, cut 10 of each shape from dough, re-rolling dough as necessary.

5 Place shapes, about 2.5cm (1-inch) apart, on trays. Bake about 15 minutes or until biscuits are firm and browned lightly. Stand biscuits on trays for 5 minutes; lift onto wire racks to cool.

6 Knead ready-made icing on surface dusted with a little cornflour until icing loses its stickiness. Divide icing into 5 equal portions. Tint each portion with one of the colourings; enclose, separately, in plastic wrap.

7 Roll each icing portion, separately, on cornfloured surface until 3mm (⅛-inch) thick. Using cutters, cut 10 teacups and 10 teapots from icings (see step 1, page 87), re-rolling icing as necessary. Reserve all icing scraps, enclose, separately, in plastic wrap.

8 Working with 2 or 3 shapes at a time, lightly, but evenly, brush tops of biscuits with egg white (see step 2, page 87); position icing shapes on biscuits.

9 Fit piping bag with tube. Fill the bag three-quarters full with royal icing; pipe outlines and lines on biscuits (see steps 3/4, page 87).

10 Re-roll icing scraps on surface dusted with cornflour until 1mm (¹⁄₃₂-inch) thick; using blossom cutters, cut 20 small and 10 large blossoms from icing. Secure 10 small blossoms to large blossoms with a little royal icing (see step 5, page 87); secure to teapot biscuits. Secure remaining small blossoms to teacup biscuits.

11 Pipe a dot of royal icing in each flower centre; using tweezers, position a pearl in centre (see step 6, page 87). Pipe dots around flowers on teapots and in teapot lids.

Continues overleaf

Step 1 Using teapot and teacup cutters, cut out shapes from the various coloured icings to match the number of biscuits.

Step 2 Working with 2 or 3 shapes at a time, brush biscuits lightly with egg white; position icing shapes on top of biscuits.

Step 3 Decorate the teacups by outlining their shape and handle with piped royal icing. Pipe vertical lines over teacup shape.

Step 4 Using piping bag and royal icing, decorate the teapots by carefully piping the outline of their shape, handle, lid and spout.

Step 5 Secure small blossoms to large blossoms with royal icing; secure to teapots. Pipe dots around blossoms and in lid area.

Step 6 Pipe dots of royal icing in centres of about four flowers; position pearls on icing. Repeat with remaining flowers and pearls.

tips You could use a paper piping bag without a tube to pipe the decorations on the biscuits. The 'pearlized blush sugar pearls' are small edible pearls, and are available from cake decorating suppliers.

Once decorated and dried, layer the biscuits carefully between sheets of baking paper in an airtight container. They will keep for about 4 weeks at room temperature. The only tricky part to making these biscuits is the piping; practise on a flat surface first, before piping onto the biscuits.

Cake pans

Step 1 To line a round cake pan, cut strips of baking paper to line the inside of the pan, overlapping slightly. Make a 2cm fold; snip paper, on an angle, up to the fold.

Step 2 Lightly grease the pan to hold the lining paper in place. Position the paper around the side of the pan, with snipped fold at the bottom.

Step 3 Trace the pan base onto baking paper. Cut paper out slightly inside the marked circle. Position in the pan to cover snipped paper.

CHOICE OF CAKE PANS

Cake pans are often measured and referred to using imperial inches - we have done the same in this book. The conversions from metric to imperial are not exact; however, this will not affect your baking. The cake charts on pages 107-113 were tested using all the different-sized pans used in this book.

Cake pans come in all shapes and sizes. Square, rectangular and octagonal shaped pans etc, have sharp corners as opposed to rounded corners; these styles of cakes are better to work with when decorating, as they start off well-shaped. We used 7.5cm (3-inch) deep cake pans with straight sides.

Cake pans are made from various metals: our chosen pans are made from a good-quality heavy tin. Aluminium pans are also good as they conduct heat evenly. We avoid pans that

have a non-stick surface or are made from flimsy metal, as cakes cooked in these tend to develop a thick crust, which can be quite tough to bite into - to counter this, reduce the oven temperature by 10 to 20 degrees.

Make sure you wash and dry cake pans thoroughly after use - drying them in a low or just-turned-off oven is a good idea. They can develop rust if they're not dried properly after use.

Before you buy a larger than normal cake pan, first measure and check that it will fit in your oven. Cakes do need a little space around them during the baking process to allow for even heat circulation. Many cake decorating shops will hire cake pans, and this is a good option if you're making a one-time-only cake.

PREPARING CAKE PANS

All cake pans must be either greased, greased and floured, or lined, to make sure the cakes don't stick. If the recipe requires a long baking time, due to the type or the size of the cake, it's vital to line the pan correctly to insulate the cake, protect the top of the cake from over-browning and to retain the shape of the cake to minimise patching and trimming, especially if the cake is to be iced and decorated.

Large cakes, over 20cm (8-inch), round or square, usually need to be baked in lined pans. The larger the cake, the more lining paper required. For added insulation, use a layer of brown paper on the outside against the side(s) of the pan, and line with baking paper on the inside of the pan. As a guide,

Step 4 Lining a square or rectangular pan is the same as for a round one. Trace the pan base onto baking paper; position over snipped paper.

Step 5 For unusual-shaped pans, use melted butter and a pastry brush to lightly, but evenly, grease the pan. Place in the fridge to set the butter.

Step 6 Sprinkle the cold, greased pan evenly with flour. Tap and turn the pan to coat the pan evenly. Invert the pan and tap to remove excess flour.

use one layer of baking paper for cakes that take less than 2 hours to bake, and three layers of baking paper for cakes that take 2 to 4 hours to bake. Use a layer of brown paper and three layers of baking paper (or greaseproof paper) for cakes needing longer than 4 hours to bake.

Lining rectangular, square, octagonal, round or oval cake pans: Cut strips of baking paper, long enough to encircle the inside of the pan, overlapping the ends slightly, and wide enough to extend 5cm (2-inches) above the side(s) of the pan. Also, allow for a fold-over at the base of the pan.

Fold 2cm (¾ inch) of the paper over, snip the paper, on an angle, up to the fold, making cuts about 1½ cm (¾ inch) apart (see step 1). Lightly grease the inside of the pan with cooking-oil spray or melted butter to hold the lining paper in place.

Position the snipped paper around the side of the pan with the snipped fold at the base of the pan (see step 2). Using the base of the pan as a guide, trace around the base on baking paper (see step 3). Cut out paper, cutting slightly inside the marked circle or square to allow for the thickness of the pan. Neatly position the paper in the pan, to cover the snipped paper (see step 4).

Preparing unusual-shaped pans: Some of the unusual-shaped pans, such as the heart pan, can't be lined efficiently. In this case, grease the pan lightly, but evenly, with melted butter, then refrigerate or freeze the pan to set the butter (see step 5). Sprinkle a little plain (all-purpose) flour all over the greased area, tap and turn the pan so that all the butter is lightly coated with flour. Turn the pan upside down over the sink or bin and knock out any excess flour (see step 6). If you prefer, line the base of the greased pan with baking paper, then just grease and flour the side(s) of the pan.

Cake boards

Step 1 Place the board on the back of the covering paper, fold sides of paper over neatly; secure with glue or tape.

Step 2 Place the board on the back of the covering paper; using scissors, snip the paper at a slight angle around the board.

Step 3 Secure snipped paper to board with glue; glue plain paper to the back of the board to cover the snipped paper.

Step 4 Use a pastry brush to evenly coat the top of a paper-covered board with sugar syrup (page 99).

Step 5 Using a rolling pin, cover the board with rolled icing. Smooth the icing with hands, then smoothing tools.

Step 6 Using a sharp knife, trim excess icing from edge of board; smooth edge(s) with fingertips.

We used wooden cake boards, as wood is strong enough to support the cakes, making them easy to handle and move. They also complement the cake, whether it's single or multi-tiered. They are available from cake decorating shops. If the cake is to be displayed on a stand, you may need to re-think the size of the base board; consider this before starting to decorate. We used imperial inches to measure the boards; the metric conversions are not exact. Covered boards can be bought from cake decorating shops. If you want to cover your own, choose a covering that is non-absorbent; cake decorating shops supply this type of paper. We used cardboard cake boards, available from cake decorating shops, for small individual cakes. Occasionally these must be trimmed to fit the base of the cake.

Covering rectangular or square boards: Cut the covering paper 5cm (2-inches) larger than the board. Place the board, top-side down, on the back of the paper (see step 1). Use tape or craft glue to stick the paper to the board. If the paper is thick, cut the corners of the paper as if covering a book. Glue a piece of paper to the back of the board to neaten the appearance.

Covering round boards: Cut the covering paper about 5cm larger than the board. Place the board, top-side down, on the back of the paper. Snip the paper border, on an angle, all the way around (see step 2). Fold snipped pieces onto the board and tape or glue in place (see step 3). Glue a piece of paper to the back of the board to neaten the appearance.

Covering boards with ready-made icing: To cover a 30cm (12-inch) board, knead 500g (1 pound) of icing on a surface dusted with a little cornflour until icing loses its stickiness. Brush the surface and the side(s) of the board with sugar syrup (see step 4). Roll the icing large enough to cover the board, about 3mm thick. Use the rolling pin to lift the icing onto the board (see step 5); smooth icing using cornfloured hands. Use smoothing tools to gently smooth the icing, easing the icing over the edge(s) of the board. Use a sharp knife to trim the icing neatly around the bottom edge(s) of the board (see step 6), then smooth the edge with your fingertip (dipped first into cornflour). Stand board for 3 hours or overnight, or until the icing is firm and dry.

Preparing cakes for covering

Step 1 Use a large sharp serrated knife to cut the rounded top off the cake so that it will sit flat when turned upside-down.

It's important cakes are properly prepared before icing. A poor covering means the cake won't stay fresh for long, and bacteria may contaminate the cake, degrading both the cake and the icing, not to mention affecting those who eat it. The cakes will keep for up to 2 weeks if covered correctly with an initial layer of ganache or almond paste, then finally covered with ready-made icing so it is airtight. Fruit and mud cakes, if covered and stored correctly, will keep for longer than other cakes. Cupcakes and smaller or cut cakes, will only keep a couple of days.

The cakes must be stored in a dust-free area at a cool room temperature. If the weather is humid, it's best to make and keep the cakes in an air-conditioned room.

Trimming cakes: Cakes must first be trimmed before any covering is applied. Most cakes need some trimming to make them flat and a good shape for decorating. We found by cooling heavy cakes, such as mud and fruit cakes, upside-down, their own weight flattens them quite a lot, and this should minimise trimming. A cake needs to sit flat and level on its board, and is almost always turned top-side down to cover with icing. After the cake has cooled and the lining paper removed, turn the cake top-side up and, using a large serrated knife, cut enough from the top of the cake (see step 1) so it sits flat when turned top-side down. Use a ruler and a small spirit level to get the cake as flat as possible; it's well worth the effort.

Step 2 Cakes need to be secured to the boards with either royal icing, softened ready-made icing or ganache – royal icing does the best job.

Securing cakes to boards: After trimming, cakes need to be secured to their boards so they can be carried safely. Royal icing anchors the cakes well, but if you're not using it to decorate the cakes, then a walnut-sized piece of ready-made icing works well, too. Knead a little cooled boiled water or sugar syrup (page 99) into the icing until it is soft and spreadable. Spread icing into the centre of the board (see step 2) then position the cake on the icing, move it around until it's where you want it (see step 3). Leave to dry out and set – it will hold the cake securely within about 24 hours.

Patching cakes: Once secured to the board, patch the cake if there are any large holes in its surface – this mainly applies to fruit cakes. Use tiny balls of ready-made icing or almond paste to fill the holes (page 98); smooth level with the cake surface, using a metal-bladed spatula, before initially covering with either almond paste, ganache or ready-made icing.

Step 3 Turn the trimmed cake upside-down; position on the royal icing as soon as it's been applied to the board. Wriggle the cake into position.

Initial covering: We prefer either ganache or almond paste for the initial covering. Alternatively, you can use just one thick layer of ready-made icing, in which case, triple the quantities of ready-made icing used to cover the cake. After the cake is trimmed, secured and patched, it is then ready for the initial covering.

Initial covering with almond paste: If a cake is to be covered with almond paste, it first needs to be brushed with sugar syrup or warmed sieved jam (page 99). This helps the paste stick to the cake's surface. The almond paste needs to be brushed again with sugar syrup so the ready-made icing covering will stick to the paste.

Initial covering with ready-made icing: You can use a thin layer of ready-made icing (about 2mm-thick) under another thin layer of ready-made icing; brush the cake with sugar syrup before applying the initial layer, then brush that layer with sugar syrup before applying the second (final) layer.

Initial covering with ganache: Apply the initial covering of ganache very thinly, then, if covering with ready-made icing, brush the ganache with sugar syrup so the icing sticks.

Ganache

Ganache is a mixture of melted chocolate and cream. It is wonderfully simple to make and versatile to use. It can be used while it's still warm as a glaze over a cake, or even as a sauce with cake. Or, let the ganache partly set, either at a cool room temperature or in the refrigerator, then beat it with a wooden spoon until it's spreadable - making it a perfect filling or frosting.

Ganache will keep in the refrigerator, covered tightly, for about two weeks (stand at room temperature to soften before use), or frozen for 3 months; thaw overnight in the refrigerator, or thaw it in the microwave oven, using short bursts of power.

Whipping ganache: Ganache can be refrigerated for around 30 minutes, or until it becomes thick and spreadable, then whipped with an electric mixer until it increases in volume and becomes fluffy, making it ideal for a frosting or filling.

Chocolate: We used dark- or milk-eating chocolate when testing the ganache recipe, use whichever type you'd be happy to eat and suits the cake. We prefer not to use cooking chocolate, but it will still work in the recipe (right). We don't use high-fat (over 70%) or low-fat chocolate.

Couverture chocolate is expensive, but the results are wonderful. It can be bought at some delicatessens and specialty food stores.

White chocolate deserves a special mention as it can be a little tricky to work with - be very careful not to overheat it or it will 'split' (turn grainy). We found that by adding more chocolate in proportion to the amount of cream (as compared to milk or dark chocolate) we got better results. Also, we found by chopping white chocolate finely, it melted faster and was less likely to split. We broke the chocolate into pieces straight into the bowl of a food processor, then processed it until finely chopped. If the ganache does split, cool it in the refrigerator, then beat the mixture with an electric mixer; this method hasn't failed us yet. See the finer points of melting chocolate on page 104.

Covering cakes with ganache: This method of using ganache as the initial covering under ready-made icing will result in a well-shaped cake that will taste good, too.

Make the ganache recipe (right). Level and trim the cake (page 91), and secure it to the board; patch the cake, if necessary (page 98), and brush lightly with sugar syrup (page 99). Spread a very, very thin coating of ganache all over the cake to hold the crumbs in place and to use as a base for the next layer of ganache (or ready-made icing or frosting). Think of this fine ganache layer as an undercoat. Stand ganache at a cool room temperature until firm to touch. (If the cake is firm, and has no crumbs, this undercoat is not necessary.)

If also using ganache as the second covering, once the undercoat is firm, lightly brush the cake again with sugar syrup, then use a metal spatula to spread a 1cm (½-inch) layer of ganache over the cake, as evenly as possible. Take your time to get the shape of the cake as perfect as possible; it's worth the effort. Use a straight-sided scraper to smooth the top and side(s) of the ganache covering. Stand the cake at a cool room temperature for about 24 hours (an air-conditioned room is perfect), or the until ganache is firm and dry to touch. If no other covering is to be applied to the ganache-covered cake, it can be refrigerated if the weather is hot, otherwise stand the cake at a cool room temperature until needed (up to a week). If refrigerated, bring the cake to room temperature before cutting and serving.

When covering a ganache undercoat with ready-made icing or frosting, brush the ganache lightly, but evenly, with sugar syrup so the icing layer will stick. Trim and neaten any rough edges from the surface of the cake so that you don't tear the ready-made icing when applying.

Note: If covering cakes with ganache then ready-rolled icing, the cake should not be refrigerated as the ganache will absorb the moisture from the fridge and transfer this to the ready-made icing, making it wet to the touch, sticky and it won't hold its shape.

White chocolate ganache

360g (11½ ounces) white eating chocolate

½ cup (125ml) pouring cream

1 Break chocolate into food processor; process until chocolate is chopped finely.
2 Bring cream to the boil in a small saucepan; remove from heat.
3 Add chocolate to cream; stir until smooth.
4 Cool mixture to room temperature if not being used as a glaze (in which case use while still warm and pourable) before beating or whipping to the desired consistency.

MAKES ENOUGH TO COVER A DEEP 20CM (8-INCH) ROUND CAKE.

Dark or milk chocolate ganache

200g (6½ ounces) milk or dark eating chocolate

½ cup (125ml) pouring cream

1 Bring cream to the boil in a small saucepan; remove from heat.
2 Break chocolate into pan with hot cream; stir until smooth.
3 Cool mixture to room temperature if not being used as a glaze (in which case use while still warm and pourable) before beating or whipping to the desired consistency.

MAKES ENOUGH TO COVER A DEEP 20CM (8-INCH) ROUND CAKE.

tips For a really impressive cake, cut it into layers, as we have done in the step shots, and top the layers with ganache, before covering the cake. You could also layer the cake with butter cream, curd, jam or any type of filling that suits the cake.

Making ganache (1) Another way to make ganache is by placing the chocolate and cream in a heatproof bowl over a saucepan of simmering water.

Making ganache (2) The heat from the water will melt the mixture, stir occasionally until smooth. The water should not touch the bottom of the bowl.

Whipped ganache Refrigerate ganache about 30 minutes, stirring occasionally, or until it becomes thick and spreadable. Beat ganache with an electric mixer until light and fluffy.

Securing cake to board (1) If ganache is the only icing being used on the cake, use a dollop to secure cake to board (or plate); spread ganache with a spatula.

Securing cake to board (2) Position cake, or a layer of a split cake, on the board (or plate). Gently push the cake layer to centre it or position it as desired.

Layering a cake with ganache Spread each layer of cake with ganache. If the weather is hot, refrigerate the layered cake before completing it.

Covering a cake with ganache (1) If covering a firm cake (with no crumbs), it doesn't need an undercoat; just spread the ganache all over the cake.

Covering a cake with ganache (2) Smooth the ganache covering all over with a scraping tool. Take your time to get the shape of the cake as perfect as possible.

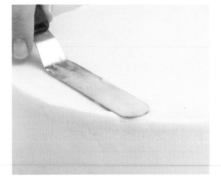

Covering a cake with ganache (3) Dip the blade of a long-bladed metal spatula into very hot water; dry. Smooth the top of the cake, reheating the blade as necessary.

Stacking & supporting tiers

Throughout this book we've used a number of stacked cakes to get the effect we wanted. Sometimes we needed to stack two deep cakes for a really impressive tall cake, other times one deep and one shallow cake stacked together gave us enough height. When stacking and joining same-sized cakes, always stack the shallow cake on top of the deep cake. The charts on pages 107-113 list the different cakes that will give you the recipes for making the correct-sized cakes. You can buy the cakes, but make sure you buy deep cakes, or you might have to stack three shallow cakes to achieve the height.

Joining uniced cakes: Cakes can be joined using either jam or ganache. Use any jam you like to join the cakes, one that will complement the flavour of the chosen cake or cakes (page 99). Sometimes it's pleasantly surprising to mix and match two or three different-flavoured cakes. If joining different-flavoured cakes, attach each cake to its own board (page 90), so that the cakes are easy to separate at serving time using a long-bladed metal spatula.

Trim the tops of the cakes to be joined, so they will sit flat on each other (page 91). Join the cut surfaces of the cakes with jam or ganache to minimise any crumbs escaping. Secure the cake to the board (page 91).

Once joined to the board(s), patch the cakes, if necessary (page 98); brush with sugar syrup and apply the initial covering of almond paste, ready-made icing or ganache and dry overnight or until dry to touch. Apply the second (final) layer to the cakes and leave overnight or until dry (this may take 2 days). You are now ready to support and stack the cakes.

Supporting tiers: Thick wooden cake skewers are used to support the weight of the upper tiers. Measure the diameter of the board under the next cake tier. Lightly mark this area in the centre of the tier below. (This is to ensure the next tier is centred on top of the bottom tier, otherwise the weight of the tiers will not be evenly distributed, which can cause heavy cakes to tilt and look unbalanced.) Insert the skewers, pointy end down (see step 1), right through to the cake board about 1cm (½ inch) in from the marked area to make neat holes in the bottom cake.

Remove the skewers, then push them into the same holes, blunt-side down, through to the board. Mark each skewer (see step 2) level with the surface of the cake tier (note which skewer came from which hole). These skewers will support the next tier, so it's important to have no gaps where the tiers join. Use strong secateurs, a hacksaw, or a strong serrated knife to cut the skewers as straight as possible (see step 3), so they are level with the top of the cake tier. Push the skewers into their correct position, cut-side down. (It's best to do this one skewer at a time, so that each skewer is returned to its original hole.) Repeat the skewering process with all the tiers, except the top tier. We use three skewers for each round cake and four skewers for each square cake between each tier. Skewers can be inserted into uniced cakes if they are to be stacked then iced (all cakes must be on boards if using skewers).

Stacking cakes: Once the skewers have been inserted into the cakes, the tiers can be stacked on top of each other. Stack and secure the next tier onto the centre of the cake below with royal icing or ready-made icing softened with some cooled boiled water (see step 4).

Carefully sit the next tier of the cake on top of the skewers (see step 5), pressing down gently to secure the bottom of the cake board to the iced cake below. Continue stacking all the tiers in the same way, being careful not to damage the covering when skewering and stacking. Fill any gaps between the tiers, where the cakes join the boards.

Filling any gaps: If a cake is to be covered with ganache or a similar frosting, gaps will be easy to cover. If the cakes are covered with ready-made icing, sometimes decorations or an edging around the tiers will cover any small gaps. To fill larger gaps, and keep the cake airtight, tint some royal icing the same colour as the icing covering the cake, and pipe a line of icing around the cake; use your finger (see step 6) to blend the icing around the cake.

At serving time, remove the top tier of the cake by sliding a long metal-bladed spatula under the board to remove it from the tier below. Remove all the skewers when cutting and serving the cake.

Note: Except for the bottom cake, which is positioned on a board that is 10cm-15cm (4-6 inches) larger than the cake (or, if being displayed on a cake stand or plate, should be positioned on a board of similar size), each tier is positioned on a wooden board that is the same size as the cake. This is to minimise any gaps between the tiers – these boards should not be visible at all.

Step 1 Push pointed ends of skewers into centre of cake right through to touch the board, keeping them straight. This makes a neat hole.

Step 2 Remove the skewers, one at a time, then push back into the cake, blunt-side down, right through to the board. Mark the skewers close to the cake surface.

Step 3 Use a serrated knife to cut the skewer at the mark; discard pointed end. Replace skewer into cake. It's best to do this one skewer at a time.

Step 4 Use a spatula to spread a dollop of royal icing (or softened ready-made icing) over the centre of the cake covering the skewered area.

Step 5 Position the next cake tier, on its board, on the icing before it sets. Centre the cake by wriggling it into position. Repeat with remaining tiers. Dry overnight.

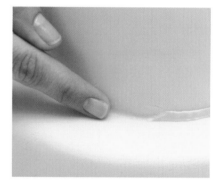

Step 6 To cover any gaps, colour royal icing to match the icing on the cake. Pipe icing around base of cake and use your fingertip to gently blend the icing into the gaps.

Transporting cakes: Tiered cakes can be very heavy – especially if fruit or mud cakes are used. Often it takes two people to carry a stacked tiered cake (and one to direct where you're walking and positioning the cake). Transporting a tiered cake can be a problem – it's large, it's heavy and you'll need to anchor the cake for its journey in the car (do not transport it on the car seat).

A thin piece of sponge rubber is usually enough to hold the cake still. Allow plenty of headroom for the cake. The only other way of handling and transporting multi-tiered cakes is to assemble the tiers at the venue. This is often impractical to do.

The *Wedding Cake Wonder* (page 72), uses a wooden dowel to secure the cakes into position. Many cake professionals use this method if the cake is three or more tiers. You can use the same technique for any cake in this book over three tiers, if you like (we used a 12mm dowel, cut to below the height of the cake). You need to drill holes through the centres of all the cake boards. You also need an undrilled wooden cake board 5cm-10cm smaller than your largest board; this is glued onto the bottom of the largest board, and is used to give height beneath the board, so you can get your fingers under it and lift it off the bench (and out of the car).

Glue the dowel into the hole in the largest board and allow to dry. The cakes (attached to their drilled boards) are pushed down over the dowel. These cakes still need to be joined with icing, stacked and supported in the usual way with skewers.

Ready-made icing

This is a great product and very forgiving for the amateur cake decorator. As with anything, you will get better at handling the icing with practise. It's available in 500g (1 pound) packets from supermarkets (usually found amongst the baking goods), and some health-food shops and delicatessens, and is found in much larger quantities from cake decorating shops. We have specified the amount of this icing you will need for each recipe. We have presumed you have initially covered the cake with either almond paste, ganache or a thin layer of ready-made icing (page 91), so we have specified only enough ready-made icing to make a thin layer over the initial covering. Should you want to use ready-made icing as the only covering on a cake, you will have to triple the quantity called for in each recipe. In most cases, cakes covered with this icing need to be left to dry for about 2 days - the time depends on the weather. If the weather is humid or wet and the icing is not drying out, put the cake in a small room, such as a bathroom or laundry, with a fan heater. Don't have the fan too hot or blowing directly onto the cake, just in case there is dust in the heater. The hot air will soon dry out the icing. If possible, work in air-conditioning when cake decorating, as it makes the processes so much easier. Some cakes in this book need to be decorated with the ready-made icing unset (still soft) so that patterns can be imprinted on it; others require it to be firm or completely set. Follow individual recipe instructions.

Colouring ready-made icing: Use good quality food colourings for best results (not the liquid dyes found in supermarkets). Always start with a tiny dab of the colouring (see step 1) - use a skewer or toothpick. Work the colour through a small ball of the icing with your fingers until it is evenly coloured. Determine the depth and strength of the colouring before adding any more and kneading it through the rest of the icing. Some cake decorating suppliers stock ready-made icings already coloured - this saves a lot of time and effort.

To cover a cake with ready-made icing: Brush the initial covering on the cake well, and evenly, with sugar syrup before you roll out the icing. Cut off as much icing as you need; re-wrap the remaining icing to exclude air or a crust will develop, which will spoil the smooth texture of the icing. Knead icing, working colouring in, on a surface dusted lightly with a little cornflour until icing is smooth and loses its stickiness. Then use a little cornflour on both the work surface and your hands, to handle the icing when rolling it out. It's important you don't use too much cornflour, as it will dry out the icing, which will cause cracks to occur in the icing when you cover the cakes. Cover any rolled icing with plastic wrap or a vinyl mat while not working with it to prevent it from drying out. Roughly measure up the side of the cake, across the top and down the other side so you have an idea of how large to roll the icing (the icing will stretch once you pick it up and while you're placing it over the cake). Use your hand to press the icing out first to a manageable thickness in the shape of the cake (circle, square), then start rolling from the centre of the icing outwards (see step 2); don't roll over the edge of the icing. Use a rolling pin to roll the icing to the correct size and thickness (about 3mm-4mm/⅛-inch, for the final cover). The icing can be rolled between sheets of baking paper, or use a non-stick mat that's suitable for rolling out icing. The mats can be bought from cake decorating shops. When rolling, try to keep the icing the shape you need, to match the shape of the cake, and the same thickness all over; do this by gently stretching and rotating the icing around as you roll. Never

Step 1 Use a toothpick or skewer to dab a little colouring onto the icing. Knead on a lightly cornfloured surface to work the colouring through evenly.

Step 2 Roll out the icing on a lightly cornfloured surface. Roll from centre to the outside edge turning and easing the icing to fit the cake.

Step 3 Gently roll icing around rolling pin. Hold the pin with one hand while supporting the icing with the other. Lift icing over cake.

turn the icing over when rolling it out. Roll the icing around the rolling pin, (see step 3) then lift the icing over the cake (see step 4). Dust your hands lightly with cornflour, and mould and smooth the icing around the shape of the cake (see step 5), gently easing out any folds in the icing. Make sure the icing feels as if it is clinging to the cake and there are no air pockets under the icing. Using the plastic smoothing tools (see step 6), smooth the edges and corners of the cakes neatly. Use a small sharp pointed knife to carefully trim away excess icing from around the base of the cake. Scraps of icing will keep well for months if they're wrapped tightly in plastic wrap to exclude the air. If you're making a tiered cake, incorporate the scraps into the next batch of icing, if they are the same colour.

If air bubbles develop in the icing during kneading, use a fine pin or fine needle to burst the bubbles, then gently smooth the icing with your fingers, the bubble and the hole from the pin will soon disappear.

Home-made icing

If you really want to make your own icing (often referred to as fondant), it's easy to make, but not as easy as buying it.

3 teaspoons powdered gelatine

2 tablespoons water

2 tablespoons glucose syrup

2 teaspoons glycerine

500g (1pound) pure icing (confectioners') sugar

1 Combine gelatine, the water, glucose and glycerine in a small saucepan. Stir over medium heat, without boiling, until gelatine is dissolved. Remove from the heat; cool until liquid is barely warm.

2 Meanwhile, finely sift icing sugar into a medium bowl. Add warm liquid; stir until mixture becomes too stiff to stir.

3 Use your hand to work ingredients into a ball, then turn the icing onto a surface dusted with more sifted icing sugar. Knead icing until smooth. Enclose icing in plastic wrap to keep airtight.

MAKES 500G (1 POUND)

tips Keep icing at a cool room temperature for 2 days, or in the fridge for 1 week. It can also be frozen for 3 months; thaw overnight in the fridge. Knead icing on a surface dusted lightly with cornflour to return it to its correct consistency.

Step 4 Gently lower the icing onto the cake surface, unrolling it from the rolling pin at the same time. The icing will stretch a little at this stage.

Step 5 Lightly cornflour your hands. Quickly smooth top of the cake, then smooth the side(s) of cake, easing the icing around the shape of the cake.

Step 6 Trim excess icing from base of the cake. Burst any air bubbles with a fine pin. Use smoothing tools to smooth icing. Neaten the cake base.

Almond paste

Almond paste, often referred to as marzipan or marzipan paste, is the traditional undercoat for rich fruit cakes, which are then usually covered with ready-made icing. Almond paste is easy to make, however, it can be bought ready-made from cake decorating suppliers, some delicatessens, supermarkets, health food shops and specialty food shops; price is a good guide to quality.

Ideally, almond-paste covered cakes need to stand for at least one day (depending on the weather – longer if the weather is humid) at room temperature to set (dry) before they are covered with ready-made icing. This gives a firm, manageable surface for the final layer. Roll out the paste on a surface lightly dusted with sifted pure icing sugar.

Covering cakes with almond paste: Trim and level the top of the cake, so it will sit flat on the board (page 91). Secure the cake to the board, top-side down. Use tiny balls of almond paste to patch any large holes in the surface of the cake; smooth the paste with a small metal-bladed spatula (see step 1). Roll thin ropes of almond paste, thick enough to fill any gaps where the cake joins the board; gently push the paste around and under the base of the cake to fill any gaps, then smooth the paste with a spatula (see step 2).

There are two methods for covering cakes with almond paste. Cakes 20cm (8-inches) or less are easily covered with one large piece of almond paste. Larger cakes are better covered using strips of almond paste for the side(s), and a square, rectangular or round shape cut-to-size, to cover the top of the cake. Brush sugar syrup over cake before covering with paste.

To cover a large cake: To cover the sides of the cake, measure up the side of the cake to determine its height then around the cake. Brush the cake all over with sugar syrup. Roll a piece of paste into a long strip, trim to fit around the side(s) of the cake; do this in about four batches, depending on the size of the cake. Position the strips of paste around the side(s) of the cake (see step 3). If you like slightly rounded corners on a square or rectangular cake, wrap strips of paste around the corners, joining strips somewhere along the side of the cake (see step 4). If you prefer sharper corners, take the strips to the corner edge, use your fingers to mould the joins together at each corner.

To cover the top of the cake, use the base of the cake pan as a guide, and roll out a piece of paste large enough to cover the top of the cake. Use your hands or a rolling pin to lift the paste into position on the cake. Use your fingers to mould the joins together. Smooth the paste with cornfloured hands (see step 5), then use the smoothing tools (see step 6) to smooth the paste. Using a small sharp knife, trim around the base of the cake to neaten.

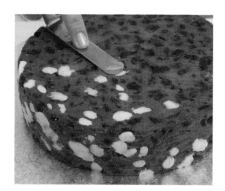

Step 1 Use small pieces of almond paste to fill and patch any holes in the cake's surface; using a metal spatula, smooth the paste level with the cake.

Step 2 Roll long thin pieces of almond paste thick enough to cover the gap around the base of the cake where it sits on the board. Smooth with a spatula.

Step 3 To cover a large cake, 22cm or more (round, square or rectangular), cut manageable strips of paste large enough to cover side(s).

Almond paste

2⅓ cups (375g) pure icing (confectioners') sugar

1 cup (125g) almond meal

2 tablespoons brandy

1 egg yolk

1 teaspoon strained lemon juice

1 Sift icing sugar and almond meal into a large bowl; discard any lumps. Stir in remaining combined ingredients.

2 When mixture becomes too stiff to stir, use your fingers to press the ingredients together. Turn paste onto surface dusted with extra sifted icing sugar; knead gently until paste becomes smooth and pliable.

3 Wrap paste in plastic wrap to keep airtight until required.

MAKES 500G (1 POUND)

tips Almond paste will keep well in the refrigerator for 2 weeks or frozen for several months. Thaw the frozen paste in the refrigerator overnight. If you're covering cakes with almond paste before ready-made icing, you will need the same quantity of almond paste as the ready-made icing specified in the recipes.

Sugar syrup

This can be bought from cake decorating shops, but it is quick, easy and inexpensive to make at home. This is used to brush onto the cake's surface before initially covering with almond paste, ready-made icing or ganache (to make them stick). The syrup is then brushed over the initial covering before the final layer of ready-made icing, or ganache, is applied.

1 cup (220g) caster (superfine) sugar

1 cup (125ml) water

1 Combine sugar and the water in a small saucepan; stir over high heat, without boiling, until sugar is dissolved.

2 Bring syrup to the boil; boil, uncovered, for 5 minutes without stirring. Cool.

3 Pour syrup into a screw-top jar, store in the fridge for up to 4 weeks.

Jam

Rather than brushing or joining the cakes with sugar syrup, you can use jams, conserves or jellies combined with complementary liqueurs or spirits instead. As a guide, for a deep 20cm (8-inch) cake you will need ¼ cup jam and 1 tablespoon liqueur (if using). Warm the jam in a small bowl over a small saucepan of simmering water; strain the jam while it's warm into another small bowl, then stir in the liqueur. Alternatively, warm the jam in a microwave safe bowl, strain it, then add the liqueur. Make sure the combinations of flavours marry well with the cake itself.

Here are some ideas:

Apricot jam and Grand Marnier or
    Cointreau or limoncello
Orange marmalade and whisky
Raspberry or strawberry jam and Framboise
Plum jam and brandy
Fig jam and rum or brandy
Redcurrant jelly and brandy

Step 4 Mould joins together with cornfloured fingers. Use the cake pan as a guide to cut out a piece of paste to cover top of the cake.

Step 5 Roll paste on a lightly cornfloured surface until large enough to cover the cake; lift paste onto cake, smooth icing over cake with hands.

Step 6 When the cake feels smooth and even, trim around the base. Use the smoothing tools to make the paste as even and as flat as possible.

Butter cream

Butter cream, also known as vienna cream, is a popular, easy-to-make frosting to use on cakes. We've left our recipe unflavoured, but if you want, you can use any extract, essence or grated citrus rind you like to flavour it. You can use either regular icing sugar (also known as icing sugar mixture or soft icing sugar - this has cornflour added to soften it) or pure icing sugar (with no added cornflour).

It's important to have the butter at room temperature, not melted or too soft. Use a small narrow mixing bowl, so that the beaters of the electric mixer can get well-down into the mixture.

The best way to cover a cake with butter cream is to spread a thin layer all over the cake, then refrigerate the cake to set the butter cream; this, in turn, will capture any loose crumbs. Apply the remaining butter cream to the cake, spreading it as evenly as possible.

Colouring the butter cream: Butter cream will always have a slightly yellow tinge to it from the butter content. This is quite tricky to counteract, especially if you want to colour the butter cream pink, as it is inclined to end up turning an apricot/salmon colour. You can buy a whitening agent from cake decorating suppliers, which will fix the problem. Beat this in before adding any colouring.

Use a skewer or toothpick to dab a tiny amount of colouring onto the butter cream (see step 1). Use a wooden spoon to mix the colouring through the butter cream evenly before adding any more. Cakes covered with butter cream can be stored in the fridge for up to 24 hours. Return the cake to room temperature before serving.

Note: Coloured butter cream will usually change colour within a few hours. It's a good idea to colour a small amount and let it stand overnight to see what happens. Some colours darken, others become lighter.

Butter cream will keep for about a week in the fridge. Allow it to come to room temperature before beating it again either with a mixer or a spoon. If it's beaten when it's too cold, it will separate. If this happens, let the mixture come to room temperature, then drain off and reserve the liquid. Beat the remaining butter mixture with an electric mixer until it becomes smooth, then beat in the reserved liquid.

Butter cream

125g (4 ounces) softened butter

1½ cups (240g) icing (confectioner's) sugar

2 tablespoons milk

1 Beat the butter (and any flavouring, if using) in a small narrow bowl with an electric mixer until the butter is as white as possible (see step 2). (This will result in a whiter butter cream, which will give you better results if colouring it.)

2 Gradually beat in half the sifted icing sugar (see step 3), then the milk, then the remaining sifted icing sugar.

3 Beat until the butter cream is smooth and spreadable. Keep scraping down the side of the bowl during beating.

To make a chocolate butter cream: Sift ⅓ cup (35g) cocoa powder in with the icing sugar.

MAKES ENOUGH TO COVER A DEEP 20CM (8-INCH) CAKE.

Step 1 Use a skewer or toothpick to dab a tiny amount of colouring onto butter cream. Use a wooden spoon to beat in the colouring.

Step 2 Beat the butter in a small narrow bowl with an electric mixer until butter is as white as possible before adding sifted icing sugar.

Step 3 Gradually beat in half the sifted icing sugar, then the milk, then remaining icing sugar. Beat until butter cream is spreadable.

Fluffy frosting

We love this frosting, it looks and tastes wonderful. It can be flavoured with any extract or essence and, because it's so white, it will happily take on any colour. We always stick to pastel colours when we use this frosting. If you want a strong-coloured frosting, however, such as red, this recipe won't work, as you need to add so much colouring that it softens the frosting, and it won't set.

Once all the syrup has been added, start beating in the colouring, a tiny dab at a time to control the colour. Scrape down the side of the bowl and the beaters to ensure the colouring is evenly distributed throughout the frosting.

We used a candy (sugar) thermometer in this recipe, but it's not essential, just boil the sugar syrup until it's thick with heavy bubbles; it should not be coloured. Remove from the heat and let the bubbles subside, then test the thickness of the syrup by dropping 1 teaspoon of it into a cup of cold water. The syrup should form a ball of soft sticky toffee.

Have the cake prepared for the frosting, as the frosting will begin to set quite quickly as it cools down. The frosting will be glossy for a few hours, then it will become dull and meringue-like in appearance and taste.

Fluffy frosting

1 cup (220g) caster (superfine) sugar
⅓ cup (80ml) water
2 egg whites

1   Stir sugar and the water in a small saucepan over high heat, without boiling, until sugar is dissolved. Boil, uncovered, without stirring, about 5 minutes or until syrup reaches 114°C/240°F on a candy thermometer (see step 1). Remove from heat, allow the bubbles to subside.

2   Begin to beat the egg whites in a small bowl with an electric mixer (see step 2) on a medium speed towards the end of the syrup's cooking time. Keep beating the egg whites while the sugar syrup reaches the correct temperature, or the egg whites will deflate.

3   With the mixer on medium speed, slowly pour in the hot syrup in a thin, steady stream (see step 3); if the syrup is added too quickly, the frosting will not thicken. Once all the syrup is added, continue beating on medium to high speed for about 10 minutes or until the mixture is thick and stands in stiff peaks; the frosting should be barely warm at this stage. Use the frosting immediately.

MAKES ENOUGH TO COVER A DEEP 20CM (8-INCH) CAKE

Using a candy thermometer: Candy thermometers must be heated to boiling point before placing into boiling syrup, otherwise the thermometer can break.

Put the thermometer into a small saucepan of cold water, bring it to the boil. When the syrup begins to boil, put the thermometer into the syrup. Leave it in the syrup until the temperature required is reached, then return it to the pan of boiling water; turn the heat off and cool the thermometer before cleaning and drying it. Digital thermometers are easier to use; they are simply placed into the boiling syrup.

When making syrup: Stir sugar and the water over heat until the sugar dissolves; any grains of sugar on the side of the pan should be brushed down into the liquid using a wet pastry brush. When the sugar is dissolved, bring the syrup to the boil; once the syrup is boiling, stop stirring. Any stirring at this point will cause the sugar to recrystallise and turn grainy, and you will have to start all over.

Step 1   Stir the sugar and the water in a pan over high heat until the sugar dissolves. Boil until the temperature reaches 114°C/240°F.

Step 2   Begin to beat the egg whites in a small bowl with an electric mixer towards the end of the cooking time of the syrup.

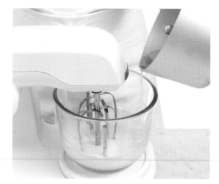

Step 3   With the mixer on medium speed, gradually pour the hot syrup into the egg whites in a thin steady stream.

Royal icing

All cake decorators mainly use royal icing for piping. It's easy to make, but a little harder to achieve the right consistency for whatever you're using it for. Using royal icing for piped flowers requires the stiffest consistency; while piping dots and lines etc, requires the softest consistency; piping basket weave, shells, stars and leaves etc, needs a medium consistency. The amount of icing sugar to use is determined by the size of the egg white and the consistency required. Getting the icing just right is a matter of experience.

We used an electric mixer for the quantity given in our recipe. Smaller quantities can be mixed in a cup using a teaspoon.

A teaspoon, or even less, of egg white is good to work with, especially for finer piping. A lot of cake decorators make royal icing by hand, not using an electric mixer, as this gives good results and minimises the development of air bubbles.

It's most important to keep this icing away from the air, as it soon develops a crust, making it unusable for piping - tiny bits of crust will block the piping tubes. Cover the surface of the icing closely with plastic wrap (see step 1), then a damp cloth, just to be sure.

Royal icing

1½ cups (240g) pure icing (confectioners') sugar, approximately

1 egg white

¼ teaspoon strained lemon juice

1 Sift the icing sugar through a fine sieve.
2 Lightly beat the egg white in a small bowl with an electric mixer until mixture is just broken up (see step 2); do not whip into peaks. Beat in the icing sugar, a tablespoon at a time, to get the required consistency.
3 When icing reaches the right consistency, mix in the lemon juice using a wooden spoon (see step 3).

tips Beat the egg whites slowly, just to break them up. You don't want to turn them into meringue, or add air bubbles – air bubbles are hard to get rid of and will affect the look of your icing and the way in which it comes out of the piping tube. An air bubble can cause a piped line of icing to break.

Sifting pure icing sugar through a very fine sieve is important, as any tiny lumps will block fine piping tubes.

If properly covered and sealed, royal icing will keep at a cool room temperature or in the fridge for several days. Beat it with a wooden spoon to bring it back to the correct consistency before using it again. Keep a wooden spoon aside just for beating royal icing. Regularly-used wooden spoons absorb fat from sweet and savoury foods, and the last thing you need in royal icing is any trace of fat.

You can buy a royal icing mix from cake decorating suppliers; this works well and is very convenient to use.

Colouring royal icing: Because the icing is white it will take on any colouring. Good quality colourings are expensive, but they are concentrated, so a little goes a long way. They are also quite stable - in other words, the colour usually doesn't change much on standing. Use a toothpick or a skewer to dab a little colouring onto the icing. Mix the colouring through with a wooden spoon, scraping down the side of the bowl often.

Step 1 Cover the surface of the icing closely with plastic wrap, then a damp cloth, to exclude air and to prevent a crust from forming on the icing.

Step 2 Beat the egg white on low speed in a small bowl just to break it up; gradually add sifted icing sugar. Beat until combined; do not whisk into peaks.

Step 3 When icing reaches the desired consistency, use a wooden spoon to stir in the juice and to break up any large air bubbles; do not whisk in more air bubbles.

Piping bags

Paper piping bags: You will find paper piping bags incredibly useful, especially if you're working with different coloured icings in small quantities. They can be used for piping ganache and butter cream as well as royal icing. You can make your own, using baking paper, or greaseproof paper, though baking paper is the stronger of the two. You can also buy large paper triangles suitable for making larger piping bags; these are available from cake decorating shops, shops that stock craft equipment and shops that supply chefs and cooks.

Basic piping used for dots, lines, loops, snail trails and so on, don't really require the use of a piping tube. Half- or three-quarters fill a paper piping bag with royal icing – whichever feels comfortable in your hand. Gently squeeze the icing down to the tip of the bag; fold the top of the bag over to enclose the icing. Use a pair of sharp scissors to snip the tiniest tip from the base of the bag, then do a test run to see if enough icing comes out of the hole to suit whatever it is you want to pipe. If not, snip another tiny piece from the bag until you get the opening just right. You can use piping tubes in these bags too; the tubes do give you more control over piped icing. If you're using piping tubes, use two thicknesses of baking paper to make the bags stronger

when piping. Follow the steps below to making paper bags – with practise you will become quick at making them in no time.

Disposable plastic piping bags: These can be bought from supermarkets in a useful medium size. You need to use piping tubes with these bags, unless you're doing some simple piped work like dots or writing (in which case, put the icing in the bag and snip the tip from the bag until the opening is of the correct size). Some boxes of bags may include a kit of a few plastic piping tubes; these are good for some piping, but not for any fine work.

Fabric piping bags: These come in a wide range of sizes, from quite small to very large. The small ones are usually used for cake decorating, either with a piping tube inserted in the opening, or fitted with a piping screw (also known as a 'coupler'), which secures the piping tube to the outside of the piping bag, making it a simple process to change tubes (to pipe a different decoration or to use the tube with a different coloured icing). Larger piping bags are usually fitted with large tubes; these are suitable for piping whipped cream, meringue and butter-based frostings. After use, wash the bags in warm water and leave to dry over a large soft-drink bottle.

Piping tubes: These are available in many sizes, either made from plastic or metal. We prefer metal tubes, they're more expensive than plastic but will last a lifetime. Wash in warm water, using a small paint brush around the tip to clean them thoroughly. Whatever you do, don't clean out leftover mixture by poking your finger through the end of the tube, as it can get stuck, which is particularly painful if it's a sharp fluted tube. Smaller diameter tubes and fluted tubes are delicate and can, with rough handling, easily become distorted, which will affect the outcome of your piping. So treat your tubes with care and store them properly.

To make a paper piping bag (1) Cut a perfect square from baking paper, fold it in half diagonally. Use a sharp knife to cut paper along the fold to make two triangles.

To make a paper piping bag (2) Hold the apex of the triangle towards you, wrap one point of the triangle around to form a cone. Wrap remaining point around to make bag.

To make a paper piping bag (3) Wriggle the points of the triangle together until they line up perfectly. Staple the bag to secure the three points in place.

Chocolate

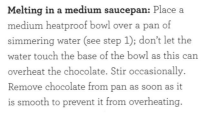

There are several ways to melt chocolate, regardless of the colour. We prefer to use a glass, china or ceramic bowl when melting chocolate over a pan of simmering water as these bowls heat slowly and melt the chocolate gently. Stainless steel bowls also work, but be aware that metal conducts heat rapidly, which can cause the chocolate to overheat if it's not watched carefully.

Seizing: This occurs when water comes in contact with the chocolate, causing it to turn hard and grainy and making it impossible to work with. You will have to start again with another batch of chocolate. It only needs the tiniest amount of water to seize.

Melting in a medium saucepan: Place a medium heatproof bowl over a pan of simmering water (see step 1); don't let the water touch the base of the bowl as this can overheat the chocolate. Stir occasionally. Remove chocolate from pan as soon as it is smooth to prevent it from overheating.

Melting in the sink: Another method that is easy and mess-free is to put the chocolate into a bowl – we used a stainless steel bowl for this method. Stand the bowl in a sink of hot tap water, or a larger bowl of hot water (see step 2). Stir occasionally until the chocolate is smooth. This method takes a little longer, but it's fail-proof. The water should come about half-way up the side of the bowl.

Melting in a microwave oven: This works a treat if you don't overheat the chocolate. Check your instruction manual for the best way. Mostly 50% or 75% power is right for melting chocolate. Place chocolate in a microwave-safe bowl (see step 3), then microwave it using short bursts of power. Check every 20 seconds by pressing it with a spatula – it could be melted even though it has retained its shape (see step 4). Don't let the tiniest drop of water near the chocolate or it will seize. Never cover or partially cover chocolate – or the bowl it is in – while it's melting, as condensation will form under the lid or covering, and drops of moisture will fall into the chocolate – and it will seize and be useless.

Step 1 To melt chocolate over a saucepan, place the chocolate in a glass bowl over a pan of simmering water; don't let water touch base of bowl; stir occasionally.

Step 2 To melt chocolate in a sink, place the chocolate in a stainless steel bowl in a sink (or a larger bowl) half-filled with hot tap water; stir occasionally.

Step 3 To melt chocolate in the microwave, place chocolate in a microwave-safe bowl; heat on medium heat. Stir often, as it holds its shape when melted.

Step 4 When microwaving chocolate, stir it regularly until smooth, as microwaved chocolate holds its shape well; test by pressing with a spoon.

Step 5 To make curls, spread melted chocolate thinly, but evenly, onto a cold surface such as marble or stainless steel; stand until almost set.

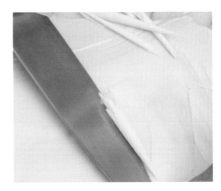

Step 6 For long thin curls, use a sharp long-bladed knife, holding the blade at a 45° angle on the surface, drag the knife over the chocolate to make curls.

Making chocolate curls: There are quite a few ways to make curls, all of which will make different-sized and shaped curls. The classic way is to spread melted chocolate evenly over a cold surface (see step 5), such as marble, a stainless steel bench top or a flat oven tray; leave it at room temperature until it is almost set; this shouldn't take long – up to 10 minutes. Drag the blade of a large sharp knife, held at about a 45 degree angle, across the chocolate to make long thin curls (see step 6). It is important the chocolate is at the right stage. If the chocolate is not set enough, it will not curl and if the chocolate is set too much, the curls will break.

If you want large chunky curls (see steps 7/8), spread melted chocolate onto a cold surface and drag an ice-cream scoop across the surface of the almost-set chocolate.

Another way to make simple small chocolate curls is to scrape a vegetable peeler along the side of a block of chocolate (see step 9). A cheese slicer is good if you want larger curls (see step 10). Make the curls from the back of a whole block of chocolate. Place the chocolate block, flat-side up, on a board and place your hand on the surface to warm it very slightly. Drag the slicer over the chocolate block. You may have to re-warm the chocolate with your hand several times during the process.

Piping chocolate: A small paper piping bag (page 103) is the best to use when piping chocolate. Cut a small snip off the end and you can pipe messages or shapes directly onto a cake, or onto baking paper – the chocolate dries quickly and can be lifted straight onto the cake. You almost always have to pipe more than you need as breakages will occur (see steps 11/12).

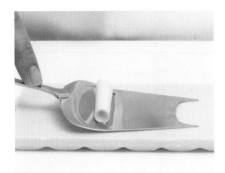

Step 7 For short chunky curls: allow the melted chocolate to almost set then hold the tip of an ice-cream scoop on the surface.

Step 8 For short chunky curls: firmly drag the ice-cream scoop over the surface of the chocolate using an even pressure.

Step 9 For smaller chocolate curls: Slightly warm the chocolate block; drag the blade of a sharp vegetable peeler evenly down the side.

Step 10 For large curls, soften back of chocolate by holding your hand on the surface for about a minute. Drag cheese slicer across chocolate.

Step 11 To pipe chocolate, first make a paper piping bag (page 103), then half-fill with melted chocolate; fold over top of bag to enclose chocolate.

Step 12 To pipe chocolate, snip a tiny tip from the paper piping bag. Pipe chocolate, holding bag at a 45° angle. Pipe freehand or use a pattern.

Making bows

Sewing a tailored bow (1): Fold a length of ribbon to make four loops. Stitch in the centre of bow to hold loops together.

Sewing a tailored bow (2): Sew a small strip of ribbon into position in the centre of the bow to cover and neaten the looped ribbon.

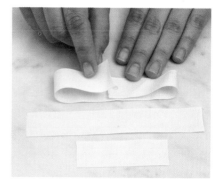

Gluing a tailored bow (1): Loop a length of ribbon bringing ends into the centre. Glue into position using a glue gun or craft glue.

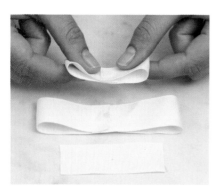

Gluing a tailored bow (2): Loop a smaller length of ribbon, secure ends in centre with glue. Glue smaller loop onto larger loop.

Gluing a tailored bow (3): Glue a small strip of ribbon over the centre of the double bow to cover and neaten the middle of the bow.

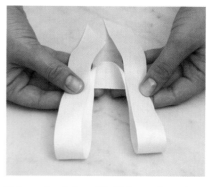

Tying a simple bow (1): Make two loops from a length of ribbon. Leave enough ribbon for tails – make these as long as you want them.

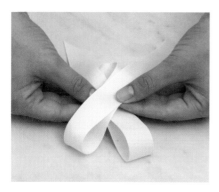

Tying a simple bow (2): Cross the loops over; bring the top loop under bottom loop then through the hole under the bottom loop.

Tying a simple bow (3): Pull the tops of the loops at the same time to make the bow even and roughly the size you want it to be.

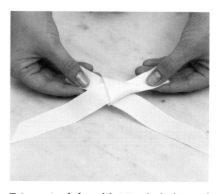

Tying a simple bow (4): Wriggle the loops of the bow until they are the same length, and the bow and its centre are as you want them.

Fruit cake

INGREDIENTS	DEEP 10CM (4-INCH) ROUND	DEEP 12CM (5-INCH) ROUND	SHALLOW 15CM (6-INCH) ROUND	DEEP 15CM (6-INCH) ROUND	DEEP 18CM (7-INCH) ROUND	SHALLOW 20CM (8-INCH) ROUND
MIXED DRIED FRUIT	320g (10oz)	480g (15½oz)	480g (15½oz)	680g (1¼lb)	1.2kg (2½lb)	500g (1lb)
MARMALADE	3 teaspoons	1 tablespoon	1 tablespoon	1 tablespoon	1½ tablespoons	7 teaspoons
DARK RUM	1½ tablespoons	2 tablespoons	2 tablespoons	¼ cup	½ cup	¼ cup
BUTTER	60g (2oz)	95g (3oz)	95g (3oz)	125g (4oz)	220g (7oz)	100g (3oz)
FINELY GRATED CITRUS RIND	½ teaspoon	½ teaspoon	½ teaspoon	1 teaspoon	1½ teaspoons	1 teaspoon
DARK BROWN SUGAR	¼ cup	⅓ cup	⅓ cup	½ cup	1 cup	½ cup
EGGS (60G/2OZ)	1	1	1	2	3	2
PLAIN (ALL-PURPOSE) FLOUR	½ cup	¾ cup	¾ cup	1 cup	1½ cups	¾ cup
MIXED SPICE	¼ teaspoon	¼ teaspoon	¼ teaspoon	½ teaspoon	1 teaspoon	¼ teaspoon
BAKING TIME (APPROX)	1¼ hours	2 hours	1½ hours	2½ hours	2½ hours	2½ hours

INGREDIENTS	DEEP 20CM (8-INCH) ROUND	SHALLOW 25CM (10-INCH) ROUND	DEEP 25CM (10-INCH) ROUND	DEEP 30CM (12-INCH) ROUND	DEEP 35CM (14-INCH) ROUND	DEEP 15CM (6-INCH) SQUARE
MIXED DRIED FRUIT	1kg (2lb)	820g (1¾lb)	2kg (4lb)	3.8kg (7½lb)	3.9kg (7½lb)	820g (1¾lb)
MARMALADE	1½ tablespoons	2 tablespoons	¼ cup	5 tablespoons	½ cup	1½ tablespoons
DARK RUM	⅓ cup	⅓ cup	¾ cup	1¼ cups	1½ cups	⅓ cup
BUTTER	200g (6½oz)	160g (5oz)	375g (12oz)	625g (1¼lb)	750g (1½lb)	160g (5oz)
FINELY GRATED CITRUS RIND	1½ teaspoons	1 teaspoon	2 teaspoons	1 tablespoon	1 tablespoon	1½ teaspoons
DARK BROWN SUGAR	¾ cup	¾ cup	1½ cups	2½ cups	3 cups	¾ cup
EGGS (60G/2OZ)	3	3	6	10	12	3
PLAIN (ALL-PURPOSE) FLOUR	1⅔ cups	1¼ cups	3 cups	5 cups	6 cups	½ cup
MIXED SPICE	1 teaspoon	¾ teaspoon	1½ teaspoons	2½ teaspoons	3 teaspoons	¾ teaspoon
BAKING TIME (APPROX)	3 hours	1½ hours	4 hours	6 hours	5 hours	2½ hours

INGREDIENTS	DEEP 20CM (8-INCH) SQUARE	DEEP 25CM (10-INCH) SQUARE	DEEP 30CM (12-INCH) SQUARE	DEEP 18CM (7-INCH) HEART SHAPED	12-HOLE MUFFIN PAN (⅓-CUP/80ML)
MIXED DRIED FRUIT	1.4kg (2¾lb)	2.4kg (4½lb)	3.9kg (7½lb)	1.4kg (2¾lb)	520g (1lb)
MARMALADE	2 tablespoons	⅓ cup	½ cup	¼ cup	2 tablespoons
DARK RUM	½ cup	1 cup	1½ cups	½ cup	¼ cup
BUTTER	250g (8oz)	460g (15oz)	750g (1½lb)	250g (8oz)	100g (3oz)
FINELY GRATED CITRUS RIND	2 teaspoons	1½ teaspoons	3 teaspoons	1 teaspoon	1 teaspoon
DARK BROWN SUGAR	1 cup	1¾ cups	3 cups	1 cup	½ cup
EGGS (60G/2OZ)	4	8	12	4	2
PLAIN (ALL-PURPOSE) FLOUR	2 cups	3¾ cups	6 cups	2 cups	¾ cup
MIXED SPICE	1 teaspoon	2 teaspoons	3 teaspoons	1 teaspoon	½ teaspoon
BAKING TIME (APPROX)	3 hours	3¼ hours	6 hours	3½ hours	50 minutes

We used 7.5cm (3-inch) deep cake pans with straight sides. Butter and eggs should be at room temperature for best results; brown sugar should be firmly packed into measuring cup. Use equal amounts of lemon and orange rind to make citrus rind. The imperial measurements are an approximation only.

1 Preheat oven to 150°C/325°F. Grease and line base and side(s) of pan (see pages 88-89).
2 Mix fruit, marmalade and rum in bowl. Beat butter, rind and sugar in another bowl with electric mixer until combined; beat in eggs, one at a time. Stir butter mixture into fruit mixture; stir in sifted flour and spice. Spread mixture into pan. Tap pan firmly on bench to settle mixture, level top of cake with wet spatula.
3 Bake cake for the time given in chart. Cover cake with foil halfway through baking if cake is over-browning, or lower the oven temperature by 10-20 degrees if cake is over 20cm.
4 Feel surface of cake; it should feel firm. Remove cake from oven, close oven door, gently push a sharp-pointed vegetable knife straight through centre of cake, right to base of pan. Withdraw knife slowly, feel blade with your fingers; if you feel uncooked mixture, return cake to oven for another 15 minutes before testing again. If the blade is free from mixture, the cake is cooked through.
5 Immediately cake is cooked, cut off paper around edge(s) of pan. Turn cake, in pan, top-side down onto foil; wrap cake and pan tightly with foil. Cover pan with a towel; cool upside down.

tips Freeze or store cake at room temperature in an airtight container well wrapped in plastic wrap. Fruit cakes will keep indefinitely; the biggest problem is insect infestation.

Butter cake

INGREDIENTS	DEEP 10CM (4-INCH) ROUND	DEEP 12CM (5-INCH) ROUND	SHALLOW 15CM (6-INCH) ROUND	DEEP 15CM (6-INCH) ROUND	DEEP 18CM (7-INCH) ROUND	SHALLOW 20CM (8-INCH) ROUND
BUTTER	45g (1½oz)	60g (2oz)	60g (2oz)	100g (3oz)	185g (6oz)	125g (4oz)
VANILLA EXTRACT	½ teaspoon	½ teaspoon	½ teaspoon	½ teaspoon	1½ teaspoons	1 teaspoon
CASTER (SUPERFINE) SUGAR	¼ cup	⅓ cup	⅓ cup	½ cup	1 cup	¾ cup
EGGS (60G/2OZ)	1	1	1	1	3	2
SELF-RAISING FLOUR	⅔ cup	¾ cup	¾ cup	1¼ cups	2¼ cups	1½ cups
MILK	¼ cup	¼ cup	¼ cup	⅓ cup	¾ cup	½ cup
BAKING TIME (APPROX)	30 minutes	40 minutes	40 minutes	50 minutes	1 hour	1 hour

INGREDIENTS	DEEP 20CM (8-INCH) ROUND	SHALLOW 25CM (10-INCH) ROUND	DEEP 25CM (10-INCH) ROUND	DEEP 30CM (12-INCH) ROUND	DEEP 35CM (14-INCH) ROUND	DEEP 15CM (6-INCH) SQUARE
BUTTER	185g (6oz)	190g (6oz)	375g (12oz)	600g (1¼lb)	1kg (2lb)	125g (4oz)
VANILLA EXTRACT	1½ teaspoons	1½ teaspoons	3 teaspoons	1 tablespoon	1 tablespoon	1 teaspoon
CASTER (SUPERFINE) SUGAR	1 cup	1¼ cups	2½ cups	3¾ cups	5 cups	¾ cup
EGGS (60G/2OZ)	3	3	6	10	14	2
SELF-RAISING FLOUR	2¼ cups	2¼ cups	4½ cups	7½ cups	12½ cups	1½ cups
MILK	¾ cup	¾ cup	1½ cups	2½ cups	4 cups	½ cup
BAKING TIME (APPROX)	1 hour	45 minutes	1½ hours	1¾ hours	2 hours	1 hour

INGREDIENTS	DEEP 20CM (8-INCH) SQUARE	DEEP 25CM (10-INCH) SQUARE	DEEP 30CM (12-INCH) SQUARE	DEEP 18CM (7-INCH) HEART SHAPED	12-HOLE MUFFIN PAN (⅓-CUP/80ML)
BUTTER	250g (8oz)	600g (1¼lb)	750g (1½lb)	125g (4oz)	185g (6oz)
VANILLA EXTRACT	2 teaspoons	1 tablespoon	1 tablespoon	1 teaspoon	1½ teaspoons
CASTER (SUPERFINE) SUGAR	1½ cups	3¾ cups	4½ cups	¾ cup	1 cup
EGGS (60G/2OZ)	4	10	12	2	3
SELF-RAISING FLOUR	3 cups	7½ cups	9 cups	1½ cups	2¼ cups
MILK	1 cup	2½ cups	3 cups	½ cup	¾ cup
BAKING TIME (APPROX)	1¼ hours	1¾ hours	2 hours	1 hour	20 minutes

We used 7.5cm (3-inch) deep cake pans with straight sides. Butter, eggs and milk should be at room temperature for best results. The imperial measurements are an approximation only.

1 Preheat oven to 180°C/350°F. Grease and line base and side(s) of cake pan with baking paper, extending paper 5cm (2 inches) above side(s) (see pages 88-89).

2 Beat butter, extract and sugar in bowl with electric mixer until light and fluffy. Beat in eggs, one at a time. Transfer mixture to larger bowl; stir in sifted flour and milk, in two batches. Spread mixture into pan.

3 Bake cake for the time given in chart. Cover cake with foil halfway through baking if cake is over-browning, or lower the oven temperature by 10-20 degrees if cake is over 20cm.

4 Test cake by inserting a skewer into centre of cake; if cooked, skewer will be clean, if there is cake mixture on the skewer, bake cake a further 10 minutes before testing again.

5 Stand cake in the pan for 10 to 30 minutes, depending on size of the cake, before turning, top-side down, onto wire rack to cool.

tip The cake will keep well for 2 days in an airtight container, or can be frozen for 3 months.

Raspberry hazelnut cake

INGREDIENTS	DEEP 10CM (4-INCH) ROUND	DEEP 12CM (5-INCH) ROUND	SHALLOW 15CM (6-INCH) ROUND	DEEP 15CM (6-INCH) ROUND	DEEP 18CM (7-INCH) ROUND	SHALLOW 20CM (8-INCH) ROUND
BUTTER	60g (2oz)	90g (3oz)	90g (3oz)	125g (4oz)	160g (5oz)	110g (3oz)
CASTER (SUPERFINE) SUGAR	½ cup	¾ cup	¾ cup	1 cup	1¼ cups	1 cup
EGGS (60G/2OZ)	1	2	2	3	4	3
PLAIN (ALL-PURPOSE) FLOUR	¼ cup	⅓ cup	⅓ cup	½ cup	⅔ cup	½ cup
SELF-RAISING FLOUR	1 tablespoon	1½ tablespoons	1½ tablespoons	¼ cup	⅓ cup	¼ cup
GROUND HAZELNUTS	¼ cup	⅓ cup	⅓ cup	½ cup	⅔ cup	½ cup
SOUR CREAM	2 tablespoons	¼ cup	¼ cup	⅓ cup	½ cup	⅓ cup
FRESH OR FROZEN RASPBERRIES	75g (2½oz)	110g (3oz)	110g (3oz)	150g (4½oz)	190g (6oz)	130g (4oz)
BAKING TIME (APPROX)	1 hour	1¼ hours	1 hour	1¼ hours	1½ hours	1 hour

INGREDIENTS	DEEP 20CM (8-INCH) ROUND	SHALLOW 25CM (10-INCH) ROUND	DEEP 25CM (10-INCH) ROUND	DEEP 30CM (12-INCH) ROUND	DEEP 35CM (14-INCH) ROUND	DEEP 15CM (6-INCH) SQUARE
BUTTER	220g (7oz)	170g (5½oz)	285g (9oz)	530g (1lb)	750g (26oz)	190g (6oz)
CASTER (SUPERFINE) SUGAR	1¾ cups	⅓ cup	2½ cups	4¼ cups	6 cups	1½ cups
EGGS (60G/2OZ)	5	4	7	13	18	4
PLAIN (ALL-PURPOSE) FLOUR	1 cup	⅔ cup	1¼ cups	2 cups	3 cups	¾ cup
SELF-RAISING FLOUR	½ cup	⅓ cup	⅔ cup	1¼ cups	1½ cups	⅓ cup
GROUND HAZELNUTS	1 cup	⅔ cup	1¼ cups	2 cups	3 cups	¾ cup
SOUR CREAM	⅔ cup	½ cup	¾ cup	1½ cups	1⅔ cups	½ cup
FRESH OR FROZEN RASPBERRIES	260g (8½oz)	210g (6½oz)	340g (11oz)	600g (1¼lb)	900g (1¾lb)	225g (7oz)
BAKING TIME (APPROX)	1¾ hours	1¼ hours	1¾ hours	1¾ hours	2½ hours	1½ hours

INGREDIENTS	DEEP 20CM (8-INCH) SQUARE	DEEP 25CM (10-INCH) SQUARE	DEEP 30CM (12-INCH) SQUARE	DEEP 18CM (7-INCH) HEART SHAPED	12-HOLE MUFFIN PAN (⅓-CUP/80ML)
BUTTER	250g (8oz)	500g (1lb)	600g (1¼lb)	250g (8oz)	90g (3oz)
CASTER (SUPERFINE) SUGAR	2 cups	4 cups	4¾ cups	2 cups	¾ cup
EGGS (60G/2OZ)	6	12	14	6	2
PLAIN (ALL-PURPOSE) FLOUR	1 cup	2 cups	2⅓ cups	1 cup	⅓ cup
SELF-RAISING FLOUR	½ cup	1 cup	1¼ cups	½ cup	1½ tablespoons
GROUND HAZELNUTS	1 cup	2 cups	2⅓ cups	1 cup	⅓ cup
SOUR CREAM	⅔ cup	1 cup	1⅔ cups	⅔ cup	¼ cup
FRESH OR FROZEN RASPBERRIES	300g (9½oz)	600g (1¼lb)	715g (1½lb)	300g (9½oz)	110g (3oz)
BAKING TIME (APPROX)	1½ hours	2¼ hours	2¼ hours	2 hours	30 minutes

We used 7.5cm (3-inch) deep cake pans with straight sides. The butter, eggs and sour cream should be at room temperature for best results. The imperial measurements are an approximation only.

1 Preheat oven to 160°C/325°F. Grease and line base and side(s) of cake pan with baking paper, extending paper 5cm (2 inches) above side(s) (see pages 88-89).

2 Beat butter and sugar in bowl with electric mixer until light and fluffy. Beat in eggs, one at a time. (Mixture will curdle at this stage but will come together later.)

3 Transfer mixture to a larger bowl; stir in the sifted flours and ground hazelnuts, sour cream and berries. Spread mixture into pan.

4 Bake cake for the time given in chart. Cover cake with foil halfway through baking if cake is over-browning, or lower the oven temperature by 10-20 degrees if cake is over 20cm.

5 Test cake by inserting a skewer into centre of cake; if cooked, skewer will be clean, if there is cake mixture on the skewer, bake cake a further 10 minutes before testing again.

6 Stand cake in the pan for 10 to 30 minutes, depending on size of the cake, before turning, top-side down, onto wire rack to cool.

tips If using frozen berries do not thaw them; frozen berries are less likely to "bleed" into the cake mixture. The cake will keep well for 3 days in an airtight container, or can be frozen for 3 months.

Coconut cake

INGREDIENTS	DEEP 10CM (4-INCH) ROUND	DEEP 12CM (5-INCH) ROUND	SHALLOW 15CM (6-INCH) ROUND	DEEP 15CM (6-INCH) ROUND	DEEP 18CM (7-INCH) ROUND	SHALLOW 20CM (8-INCH) ROUND
BUTTER	80g (2½oz)	85g (3oz)	85g (3oz)	125g (4oz)	180g (5½oz)	150g (4½oz)
COCONUT ESSENCE	½ teaspoon	1 teaspoon	¾ teaspoon	1 teaspoon	1½ teaspoons	1 teaspoon
CASTER (SUPERFINE) SUGAR	¾ cup	⅔ cup	⅔ cup	1 cup	1½ cups	1¼ cups
COCONUT CREAM	½ cup	½ cup	½ cup	¾ cup	1 cup	1 cup
SELF-RAISING FLOUR	⅔ cup	¾ cup	¾ cup	1 cup	1⅔ cups	1⅓ cups
EGG WHITES	2	2	2	3	4	4
BAKING TIME (APPROX)	50 minutes	1½ hours	50 minutes	1½ hours	1½ hours	1 hour

INGREDIENTS	DEEP 20CM (8-INCH) ROUND	SHALLOW 25CM (10-INCH) ROUND	DEEP 25CM (10-INCH) ROUND	DEEP 30CM (12-INCH) ROUND	DEEP 35CM (14-INCH) ROUND	DEEP 15 CM (6-INCH) SQUARE
BUTTER	295g (9½oz)	250g (8oz)	375g (12oz)	670g (1¼lb)	830g (1¾lb)	170g (5½oz)
COCONUT ESSENCE	2 teaspoons	2 teaspoons	3 teaspoons	1 tablespoon	1 tablespoon	1 teaspoon
CASTER (SUPERFINE) SUGAR	2⅓ cups	2 cups	3 cups	5⅓ cups	6⅔ cups	1⅓ cups
COCONUT CREAM	1¾ cups	1½ cups	2¼ cups	4 cups	5 cups	1 cup
SELF-RAISING FLOUR	2⅔ cups	2¼ cups	3⅓ cups	6 cups	7½ cups	1½ cups
EGG WHITES	7	6	9	16	20	4
BAKING TIME (APPROX)	1¾ hours	1¼ hours	1½ hours	2¼ hours	3 hours	1½ hours

INGREDIENTS	DEEP 20CM (8-INCH) SQUARE	DEEP 25CM (10-INCH) SQUARE	DEEP 30CM (12-INCH) SQUARE	DEEP 18CM (7-INCH) HEART SHAPED	12-HOLE MUFFIN PAN (⅓-CUP/80ML)
BUTTER	250g (8oz)	500g (1lb)	830g (1¾lb)	250g (8oz)	150g (4½oz)
COCONUT ESSENCE	2 teaspoons	1 tablespoon	1 tablespoon	2 teaspoons	1 teaspoon
CASTER (SUPERFINE) SUGAR	2 cups	4 cups	6⅔ cups	2 cups	1¼ cups
COCONUT CREAM	1½ cups	3 cups	5 cups	1½ cups	1 cup
SELF-RAISING FLOUR	2¼ cups	4½ cups	7½ cups	2¼ cups	1⅓ cups
EGG WHITES	6	12	20	6	4
BAKING TIME (APPROX)	1 hour	1½ hours	3 hours	45 minutes	45 minutes

We used 7.5cm (3-inch) deep cake pans with straight sides. Butter and egg whites should be at room temperature for best results. We used canned coconut cream. The imperial measurements are an approximation only.

1   Preheat oven to 160°C/325°F. Grease and line base and side(s) of cake pan with baking paper, extending paper 5cm (2 inches) above side(s) (see pages 88-89).

2   Beat butter, essence and sugar in bowl with electric mixer until light and fluffy. Transfer mixture to a larger bowl; stir in coconut cream and sifted flour, in two batches.

3   Beat egg whites in bowl (see tips) with electric mixer until soft peaks form. Fold egg whites into coconut mixture, in two batches. Spread mixture into pan.

4   Bake cake for the time given in chart. Cover cake with foil halfway through baking if cake is over-browning, or lower the oven temperature by 10-20 degrees if cake is over 20cm.

5   Test cake by inserting a skewer into centre of cake; if cooked, skewer will be clean, if there is cake mixture on the skewer, bake cake a further 10 minutes before testing again. Cool cake in pan.

tips   The egg whites need to be beaten in a narrow bowl so that the beaters are well down in the egg whites to create the necessary volume. If beating large quantities of egg whites, say, more than 10, beat them in 2 or more batches. This cake is quite soft, and needs to be cooled in the pan before turning out. The cake will keep well for 3 days in an airtight container, or it can be frozen for 3 months.

Carrot cake

INGREDIENTS	DEEP 10CM (4-INCH) ROUND	DEEP 12CM (5-INCH) ROUND	SHALLOW 15CM (6-INCH) ROUND	DEEP 15CM (6-INCH) ROUND	DEEP 18CM (7-INCH) ROUND	SHALLOW 20CM (8-INCH) ROUND
SELF-RAISING FLOUR	½ cup	⅓ cup	½ cup	½ cup	1 cup	1 cup
PLAIN (ALL-PURPOSE) FLOUR	¼ cup	¼ cup	⅓ cup	⅓ cup	⅔ cup	½ cup
BICARBONATE OF SODA	¼ teaspoon	¼ teaspoon	½ teaspoon	½ teaspoon	½ teaspoon	½ teaspoon
MIXED SPICE	1 teaspoon	1 teaspoon	1 teaspoon	1 teaspoon	3 teaspoons	2 teaspoons
LIGHT BROWN SUGAR	¼ cup	¼ cup	⅓ cup	⅓ cup	⅔ cup	½ cup
COARSELY GRATED CARROT	¾ cup	¾ cup	1 cup	1 cup	2 cups	1½ cups
VEGETABLE OIL	¼ cup	¼ cup	⅓ cup	⅓ cup	⅔ cup	½ cup
EGGS (60G/2OZ)	1	1	1	1	3	2
SOUR CREAM	¼ cup	¼ cup	⅓ cup	⅓ cup	⅔ cup	½ cup
BAKING TIME (APPROX)	1 hour	1 hour	30 minutes	1 hour	1½ hours	1 hour

INGREDIENTS	DEEP 20CM (8-INCH) ROUND	SHALLOW 25CM (10-INCH) ROUND	DEEP 25CM (10-INCH) ROUND	DEEP 30CM (12-INCH) ROUND	DEEP 35CM (14-INCH) ROUND	DEEP 15CM (6-INCH) SQUARE
SELF-RAISING FLOUR	1 cup	1½ cups	1¾ cups	3 cups	5 cups	¾ cup
PLAIN (ALL-PURPOSE) FLOUR	⅔ cup	1 cup	1¼ cups	2 cups	3¼ cups	½ cup
BICARBONATE OF SODA	½ teaspoon	1 teaspoon	1¼ teaspoons	2 teaspoons	3 teaspoons	½ teaspoon
MIXED SPICE	3 teaspoons	1 tablespoon	1 tablespoon	2 tablespoons	2 tablespoons	2 teaspoons
LIGHT BROWN SUGAR	⅔ cup	1 cup	1¼ cups	2 cups	3¼ cups	½ cup
COARSELY GRATED CARROT	2 cups	3 cups	3¾ cups	6 cups	8¼ cups	1½ cups
VEGETABLE OIL	⅔ cup	1 cup	1¼ cups	2 cups	3¼ cups	½ cup
EGGS (60G/2OZ)	3	4	5	8	13	2
SOUR CREAM	⅔ cup	1 cup	1¼ cups	2 cups	3¼ cups	½ cup
BAKING TIME (APPROX)	1½ hours	1¾ hours	2 hours	2½ hours	2 hours	1¼ hours

INGREDIENTS	DEEP 20CM (8-INCH) SQUARE	DEEP 25CM (10-INCH) SQUARE	DEEP 30CM (12-INCH) SQUARE	DEEP 18CM (7-INCH) HEART SHAPED	12-HOLE MUFFIN PAN (⅓-CUP/80ML)
SELF-RAISING FLOUR	1½ cups	3 cups	3¾ cups	1½ cups	¾ cup
PLAIN (ALL-PURPOSE) FLOUR	1 cup	2 cups	2½ cups	1 cup	½ cup
BICARBONATE OF SODA	1 teaspoon	2 teaspoons	2 teaspoons	1 teaspoon	½ teaspoon
MIXED SPICE	1 tablespoon	2 tablespoons	2 tablespoons	1 tablespoon	2 teaspoons
LIGHT BROWN SUGAR	1 cup	2 cups	2½ cups	1 cup	½ cup
COARSELY GRATED CARROT	3 cups	6 cups	7½ cups	3 cups	1½ cups
VEGETABLE OIL	1 cup	2 cups	2½ cups	1 cup	½ cup
EGGS (60G/2OZ)	4	8	10	4	2
SOUR CREAM	1 cup	2 cups	2½ cups	1 cup	½ cup
BAKING TIME (APPROX)	1¾ hours	1¾ hours	3 hours	1¾ hours	45 minutes

We used 7.5cm (3-inch) deep cake pans with straight sides. Eggs and sour cream should be at room temperature for best results. Brown sugar and carrot should be firmly packed into measuring cup(s). The imperial measurements are an approximation only.

1 Preheat oven to 160°C/325°F. Grease and line base and side(s) of cake pan with baking paper, extending paper 5cm (2 inches) above side(s) (see pages 88-89).

2 Sift flours, soda, spice and sugar into bowl. Add carrot; stir in combined oil, eggs and sour cream (do not over-mix). Spread mixture into pan.

3 Bake cake for the time given in chart. Cover cake with foil halfway through baking if cake is over-browning, or lower the oven temperature by 10-20 degrees if cake is over 20cm.

4 Test cake by inserting a skewer into centre of cake; if cooked, skewer will be clean, if there is cake mixture on the skewer, bake cake a further 10 minutes before testing again.

5 Stand cake in the pan for 10 to 30 minutes, depending on size of the cake, before turning, top-side down, onto wire rack to cool.

tip The cake will keep well for 5 days in an airtight container, or can be frozen for 3 months.

White chocolate mud cake

INGREDIENTS	DEEP 10CM (4-INCH) ROUND	DEEP 12CM (5-INCH) ROUND	SHALLOW 15CM (6-INCH) ROUND	DEEP 15CM (6-INCH) ROUND	DEEP 18CM (7-INCH) ROUND	SHALLOW 20CM (8-INCH) ROUND
BUTTER	85g (3oz)	85g (3oz)	105g (3½oz)	125g (4oz)	250g (8oz)	165g (5oz)
WHITE EATING CHOCOLATE	45g (1½oz)	45g (1½oz)	60g (2oz)	75g (2½oz)	150g (4½oz)	100g (3oz)
CASTER (SUPERFINE) SUGAR	⅔ cup	⅔ cup	⅔ cup	1 cup	2 cups	1⅓ cups
MILK	⅓ cup	⅓ cup	½ cup	½ cup	1 cup	⅔ cup
PLAIN (ALL-PURPOSE) FLOUR	½ cup	½ cup	¾ cup	¾ cup	1½ cups	1 cup
SELF-RAISING FLOUR	2 tablespoons	2 tablespoons	¼ cup	¼ cup	½ cup	⅓ cup
VANILLA EXTRACT	¼ teaspoon	¼ teaspoon	½ teaspoon	½ teaspoon	1 teaspoon	½ teaspoon
EGGS (60G/2OZ)	1	1	1	1	2	1
BAKING TIME (APPROX)	1¼ hours	1¼ hours	1 hour	1½ hours	1¾ hours	1¼ hours

INGREDIENTS	DEEP 20CM (8-INCH) ROUND	SHALLOW 25CM (10-INCH) ROUND	DEEP 25CM (10-INCH) ROUND	DEEP 30CM (12-INCH) ROUND	DEEP 35CM (14-INCH) ROUND	DEEP 15CM (6-INCH) SQUARE
BUTTER	250g (8oz)	290g (9oz)	375g (12oz)	600g (1¼lb)	1.2kg (2½lb)	165g (5oz)
WHITE EATING CHOCOLATE	150g (4½oz)	175g (5½oz)	225g (7oz)	375g (12oz)	800g (1½lb)	100g (3oz)
CASTER (SUPERFINE) SUGAR	2 cups	2⅓ cups	3 cups	5 cups	10 cups	1⅓ cups
MILK	1 cup	1¼ cups	1½ cups	2½ cups	5 cups	⅔ cup
PLAIN (ALL-PURPOSE) FLOUR	1½ cups	1¾ cups	2¼ cups	3¾ cups	8 cups	1 cup
SELF-RAISING FLOUR	½ cup	¾ cup	¾ cup	1¼ cups	2½ cups	⅓ cup
VANILLA EXTRACT	1 teaspoon	1 teaspoon	1½ teaspoons	2½ teaspoons	1 tablespoon	½ teaspoon
EGGS (60G/2OZ)	2	3	3	5	10	1
BAKING TIME (APPROX)	1¾ hours	1¾ hours	2½ hours	3½ hours	4½ hours	1¾ hours

INGREDIENTS	DEEP 20CM (8-INCH) SQUARE	DEEP 25CM (10-INCH) SQUARE	DEEP 30CM (12-INCH) SQUARE	DEEP 18CM (7-INCH) HEART SHAPED	12-HOLE MUFFIN PAN (⅓-CUP/80ML)
BUTTER	335g (10½oz)	500g (1lb)	750g (1½lb)	335g (10½oz)	250g (8oz)
WHITE EATING CHOCOLATE	200g (6½oz)	300g (9½oz)	450g (14½oz)	200g (6½oz)	150g (4½oz)
CASTER (SUPERFINE) SUGAR	2⅔ cups	4 cups	6 cups	2⅔ cups	2 cups
MILK	1½ cups	2 cups	3 cups	1½ cups	1 cup
PLAIN (ALL-PURPOSE) FLOUR	2 cups	3 cups	4½ cups	2 cups	1½ cups
SELF-RAISING FLOUR	⅔ cup	1 cup	1½ cups	⅔ cup	½ cup
VANILLA EXTRACT	1 teaspoon	2 teaspoons	3 teaspoons	1 teaspoon	1 teaspoon
EGGS (60G/2OZ)	3	4	6	3	2
BAKING TIME (APPROX)	2 hours	3 hours	4 hours	2 hours	50 minutes

We used 7.5cm (3-inch) deep cake pans with straight sides. Eggs should be at room temperature for best results. The imperial measurements used here are an approximation only.

1 Preheat oven to 160°C/325°F. Grease and line base and side(s) of cake pan with baking paper, extending paper 5cm (2 inches) above side(s) (see pages 88-89).

2 Combine chopped butter, broken chocolate, sugar and milk in a saucepan; stir over low heat until mixture is smooth. Transfer mixture to a bowl; cool 15 minutes.

3 Whisk in sifted flours, extract and lightly beaten eggs. Pour mixture into pan.

4 Bake the cake for the time given in chart. Cover cake with foil halfway through baking if the cake is over-browning, or lower the oven temperature by 10-20 degrees if cake is over 20cm.

5 Cake will develop a thick sugary crust during baking (cracks are normal); test for firmness by touching with fingers about 5 minutes before the end of baking time, then, test with a skewer. If cooked, skewer will be clean, if there is cake mixture on the skewer, bake cake a further 10 minutes before testing again. Cool cake in pan.

tip The cake will keep well for 1 week in an airtight container, or can be frozen for 3 months.

Dark chocolate mud cake

INGREDIENTS	DEEP 10CM (4-INCH) ROUND	DEEP 12CM (5-INCH) ROUND	SHALLOW 15CM (6-INCH) ROUND	DEEP 15CM (6-INCH) ROUND	DEEP 18CM (7-INCH) ROUND	SHALLOW 20CM (8-INCH) ROUND
BUTTER	125g (4oz)	125g (4oz)	125g (4oz)	175g (5½oz)	240g (7½oz)	225g (7oz)
DARK EATING CHOCOLATE	185g (6oz)	185g (6oz)	185g (6oz)	270g (8½oz)	375g (12oz)	360g (11½oz)
INSTANT COFFEE GRANULES	2 teaspoons	2 teaspoons	2 teaspoons	3 teaspoons	1 tablespoon	1 tablespoon
WATER	⅓ cup	⅓ cup	⅓ cup	½ cup	⅔ cup	¾ cup
LIGHT BROWN SUGAR	⅓ cup	⅓ cup	⅓ cup	½ cup	⅔ cup	¾ cup
PLAIN (ALL-PURPOSE) FLOUR	½ cup	½ cup	½ cup	¾ cup	1 cup	1 cup
SELF-RAISING FLOUR	2 tablespoons	2 tablespoons	2 tablespoons	¼ cup	¼ cup	¼ cup
EGGS (60G/2OZ)	1	1	1	1	2	2
COFFEE-FLAVOURED LIQUEUR	2 tablespoons	2 tablespoons	2 tablespoons	¼ cup	¼ cup	¼ cup
BAKING TIME (APPROX)	1 hour	1½ hours	1½ hours	1¾ hours	2 hours	2 hours

INGREDIENTS	DEEP 20CM (8-INCH) ROUND	SHALLOW 25CM (10-INCH) ROUND	DEEP 25CM (10-INCH) ROUND	DEEP 30CM (12-INCH) ROUND	DEEP 35CM (14-INCH) ROUND	DEEP 15CM (6-INCH) SQUARE
BUTTER	395g (12½oz)	395g (12½oz)	525g (1lb)	900g (1¾lb)	1.4kg (2¾lb)	250g (8oz)
DARK EATING CHOCOLATE	625g (1¼lb)	625g (1¼lb)	840g (1¾lb)	1.5kg (3lb)	2.3kg (4½lb)	185g (6oz)
INSTANT COFFEE GRANULES	1½ tablespoons	1½ tablespoons	2 tablespoons	⅓ cup	⅓ cup	2 teaspoons
WATER	1 cup	1 cup	1¼ cups	2⅔ cups	4 cups	⅓ cup
LIGHT BROWN SUGAR	1 cup	1 cup	1¼ cups	2⅔ cups	4 cups	⅓ cup
PLAIN (ALL-PURPOSE) FLOUR	1½ cups	1½ cups	1¾ cups	3½ cups	5½ cups	½ cup
SELF-RAISING FLOUR	⅓ cup	⅓ cup	½ cup	1 cup	1⅓ cups	2 tablespoons
EGGS (60G/2OZ)	3	3	4	7	11	1
COFFEE-FLAVOURED LIQUEUR	⅓ cup	⅓ cup	⅓ cup	1 cup	1⅓ cups	¼ cup
BAKING TIME (APPROX)	2¼ hours	2 hours	2½ hours	4 hours	3 hours	1¼ hours

INGREDIENTS	DEEP 20CM (8-INCH) SQUARE	DEEP 25CM (10-INCH) SQUARE	DEEP 30CM (12-INCH) SQUARE	DEEP 18CM (7-INCH) HEART SHAPED	12-HOLE MUFFIN PAN (⅓-CUP/80ML)
BUTTER	430g (14oz)	550g (1lb)	1kg (2lb)	395g (12½oz)	225g (7oz)
DARK EATING CHOCOLATE	675g (1¼lb)	920g (1¾lb)	1.7kg (3½lb)	625g (1¼lb)	360g (11½oz)
INSTANT COFFEE GRANULES	1½ tablespoons	2 tablespoons	⅓ cup	1½ tablespoons	1 tablespoon
WATER	1¼ cups	1⅔ cups	3 cups	1 cup	¾ cup
LIGHT BROWN SUGAR	1¼ cups	1⅔ cups	3 cups	1 cup	¾ cup
PLAIN (ALL-PURPOSE) FLOUR	1¾ cups	2¼ cups	4 cups	1½ cups	1 cup
SELF-RAISING FLOUR	½ cup	½ cup	1 cup	⅓ cup	¼ cup
EGGS (60G/2OZ)	4	4	8	3	2
COFFEE-FLAVOURED LIQUEUR	⅓ cup	½ cup	1 cup	⅓ cup	¼ cup
BAKING TIME (APPROX)	2½ hours	2¼ hours	4½ hours	1½ hours	50 minutes

We used 7.5cm (3-inch) deep cake pans with straight sides. Eggs should be at room temperature for best results. Light brown sugar should be firmly packed into the measuring cup(s). Use soft light brown sugar in this recipe, not soft dark brown or raw sugar. Imperial measurements are an approximation only.

1 Preheat oven to 160°C/325°F. Grease and line base and side(s) of cake pan with baking paper, extending paper 5cm (2 inches) above side(s) (see pages 88-89).
2 Combine chopped butter, broken chocolate, coffee, the water and sugar in saucepan; stir over low heat until smooth. Transfer mixture to bowl; cool 15 minutes. Whisk in sifted flours, lightly beaten eggs and liqueur. Pour mixture into pan.
3 Bake cake for the time given in chart. Cover cake with foil halfway through baking if cake is over-browning, or lower the oven temperature by 10-20 degrees if cake is over 20cm.

4 Cake will develop a thick sugary crust during baking (cracks are normal); test for firmness by touching with fingers about 5 minutes before the end of baking time, then, test with a skewer. If cooked, skewer will be clean, if there is cake mixture on the skewer, bake a further 10 minutes before testing again. Cool cake in pan.

tip The cake will keep well for 1 week in an airtight container, or can be frozen for 3 months.

GLOSSARY

ALMOND MEAL also known as ground almonds; nuts are powdered to a coarse flour-like texture.

ALMOND PASTE similar to marzipan, but is less granular and contains less sugar (see also marzipan).

BAKING PAPER (parchment paper or baking parchment) a silicone-coated paper primarily used for lining baking pans and trays so cakes and biscuits won't stick, making removal easy.

BAKING POWDER a raising agent consisting of two parts cream of tartar to one part bicarbonate of soda.

BALL TOOL a plastic stick with a ball of different sizes at either end. Is used to thin ready-made icing when making flower petals, and to smooth curves and rounded ends. There are a number of sizes available.

BICARBONATE OF SODA also known as baking or carb soda; is used as a leavening (raising) agent in baking.

BLOSSOM CUTTERS tiny cutters used to make small flowers; come as 3, 4 or 5 petals (see also flower cutters).

BRUSHES artist's paint brushes and make-up brushes are excellent when brushing cakes, models, flowers and myriad other decorations with glitter, powder or dusts, or painting colours, water or sugar syrup onto cakes. Larger-sized brushes are also useful for brushing crumbs off cakes or dried icing from boards.

BUTTER use salted or unsalted (sweet) butter; 125g is equal to one stick (4oz) of butter.

CACHOUS also known as dragées; these minuscule (3mm to 5mm) metallic-looking-but-edible confectionery balls are available in silver, gold or various colours.

CAKE BOARDS often made from masonite and covered in a thick non-absorbable paper, silver or gold coloured. Come in myriad sizes, usually round or square, occasionally octagonal. If displaying on a cake board, rather than a plate, the base board is often 10-15cm larger than the cake, so it can be lifted and transported without fingers poking holes in the icing. The remaining cakes are placed on cake boards of the same size. If displaying on a cake plate, the base board should be the same size as the cake.

CHOCOLATE
dark eating also known as semi-sweet or luxury chocolate; made of a high percentage of cocoa liquor, cocoa butter, and a little added sugar.
milk mild and very sweet; similar in make-up to dark with the difference being the addition of milk solids.
white contains no cocoa solids but derives its sweet flavour from cocoa butter. Very sensitive to heat so watch carefully when melting.

COCOA POWDER also known as cocoa; dried, unsweetened, roasted and ground cocoa beans (cacao seeds). dutch cocoa is treated with an alkali to neutralise its acids. It has a reddish-brown colour, a mild flavour and is easy to dissolve in liquids.

COCONUT
desiccated dried, unsweetened, finely shredded coconut.
essence produced from coconut flavouring, oil and alcohol.
flaked dried, flaked coconut flesh.
shredded strips of dried coconut.

CORNFLOUR (cornstarch) often used as a thickener, here we use it to roll out ready-made icing and modelling paste.

COUPLER this device lets you quickly change piping tubes without changing the bag. It has two parts; the base sits on the inside of the bag with the end poking out; the piping tube is then placed over the part poking out and the ring is twisted or screwed over the tube to lock it in place.

CREAM we use fresh cream, also known as pouring, single and pure cream, unless otherwise stated. It has no additives, unlike commercially thickened cream, and has a minimum fat content of 35%.
sour a thick cultured soured cream. Minimum fat content 35%.

CREAM CHEESE commonly known as Philadelphia or Philly, a soft cow's-milk cheese with a fat content of at least 33%.

CREAM OF TARTAR an acid ingredient in baking powder; keeps frostings creamy and improves volume when beating egg whites. Helps prevent sugar from crystallising when added to confectionery mixtures.

CUTTERS come in many sizes, shapes, styles, plunging etc. Used to cut ready-made icing and modelling paste into different shapes.

EDIBLE DUST, GLITTER, POWDERS are available from cake decorating suppliers. Used to add details and highlights to cakes.

EMBOSSING TOOLS are pressed or rolled onto soft ready-made icing leaving a print of the design. Textured mats are also a type of embossing tool.

FILIGREE an intricate type of lace work done using royal icing. Is very delicate and breaks easily.

FLORAL WIRE also known as florist's or craft wire. A covered flexible wire that comes in different thicknesses. The higher the number of the gauge (eg 33-gauge) the finer the wire and the finer the wire the more delicate and flexible it is (used for smaller pieces); the lower the number of the gauge (eg 18-gauge) the thicker the wire (used for making large sugar flowers). Also used to bind petals when making flowers, or to position shapes or flowers into cakes. The wire itself may be uncovered or wrapped in white or green florist's tape. Available from craft and cake decorating suppliers in cut lengths (36cm/14½ inches) and on spools. When we ask for a length of wire, we mean 36cm lengths.

FLORIST'S TAPE from craft and cake decorating suppliers. Wrapped around flower stems to provide a seal when placing fresh flowers on cakes. Also used to cover wooden dowels, or to cover floral wire when making flowers from modelling paste, etc, to hold the petals in place.

FLOUR
plain a general all-purpose flour made from wheat.
rice very fine, almost powdery, flour; made from ground white rice (this flour is gluten-free).
self-raising plain flour sifted with baking powder in the proportion of 1 cup flour to 2 teaspoons baking powder. Also called self-rising flour.

FLOWER CUTTERS used to cut small flower shapes (see also blossom cutters).

FLOWER MAT also known as foam pad and celpad. Provides a soft surface when working with ready-made icing and modelling paste to make flower petals, etc. Provides a soft base when pushing cutouts out of plunger cutters.

FLOWER SPIKES are hollow plastic spikes that are pushed through the icing into the cake. Used to position wired flowers and other decorations, thus keeping the floral wire out of the cake. This is a safe, hygienic way to add embellishments to the cake. Fresh flowers can also be positioned in spikes; add a couple of drops of water into the spike to keep the flowers fresh during the celebration.

FOOD COLOURING dyes used to change the colour of foods.
concentrated pastes, which is what we used throughout this book, are the easiest to use, though are a little more expensive.
liquid dyes the strength varies depending on the quality. Useful for pastel colours only, as adding large amounts of liquid colouring will break down most icings. Also useful for painting icing sculptures.

powdered colourings are best for primary colours or black.

FRILLING TOOL usually comes as part of a 'modelling' kit. Used to frill the edges of ready-made icing.

GELATINE a thickening agent. Comes in sheet form, known as leaf gelatine, or as a powder. Three teaspoons of powdered gelatine (7g or one sachet) is roughly equivalent to four gelatine leaves. We used powdered gelatine.

GLUCOSE SYRUP also known as liquid glucose; a clear, thick liquid often made from wheat or corn starch.

GLYCERINE a sweet and colourless liquid that retains moisture and adds sweetness to cakes. It also softens ready-made and royal icings.

GOLDEN SYRUP a by-product of refined sugarcane; pure maple syrup or honey can be substituted.

HAZELNUTS also known as filberts; a plump, grape-sized, rich, sweet nut.
meal known as ground hazelnuts.

JAM also known as preserve or conserve; most often made from fruit. When heated and mixed with a little water, it can be used as a glaze to cover cakes, this acts as a glue helping the initial covering of the cake stick to the cake's surface. Strain the jam mixture before spreading over the cake to remove any solid pieces of fruit.

MARZIPAN an almond and sugar paste used to cover cakes, as a filling in danish pastries or sculpted into a variety of shapes to be eaten as candy or used as cake decorations. After kneading, it has the consistency of dough and can be rolled, shaped, cut or moulded (see also almond paste).

METAL SPATULA also known as a palette knife. Come in small, medium and large. The larger ones have flexible steel blades. There are two types, straight-bladed, and offset or crank, which is used for getting into tight areas the flat straight blade can't.

MIXED FRUIT consists of a mixture of sultanas, raisins, currants, mixed peel and sometimes glacé cherries.

MIXED SPICE a blend of ground spices usually consisting of cinnamon, allspice and nutmeg.

MODELLING PASTE also known as BAS relief paste, gum paste, flower modelling paste and pastillage. Sets very hard, and is used to make all types of decorations for cakes.

MODELLING TOOLS are used to draw, frill, shape, imprint, stencil, hollow or cut soft icing when making decorations for cakes. Can be found singly, but are also available in kits.

MUSLIN a loosely-woven cotton fabric. Tie cornflour in a square of muslin and use to lightly dust the bench when kneading and rolling ready-made icing.

NOUGAT a confectionery made from honey, nuts and egg whites. The nougat we are most familiar with is the chewy white confectionery studded with nuts, however, it can be either soft and chewy or crunchy.

NUTMEG dried nut of an evergreen tree native to Indonesia; it is available in ground form or you can grate your own with a fine grater.

PERSPEX MEASURES these are clear rulers that come in different widths; used to cut icing ribbons to specified widths for cakes. Often come in a set of 5 widths.

PETAL CUTTERS are various metal or plastic cutters that come in the shape of flower petals. Available as a kit for specific flowers, which also include the veining tool.

PIPING BAGS
disposable bags are made of clear plastic. Discard after each use. Only available in one size and come in packs; available from supermarkets.
paper piping bags are made from baking paper (silicone or parchment paper) and discarded after each use. Used for small amounts of icing, writing, flooding (runouts), etc. See page 103 for directions on how to make them.
polyester bags are lightweight, flexible and reusable. Wash in hot soapy water after each use and dry, standing over a soft drink bottle. Are available in many different sizes.

PIPING TUBES small metal or plastic cone shapes with various openings used to produce many different designs when icing or frosting is pressed through them. Smaller ones are quite fragile and must be treated carefully, otherwise they can be bent or squashed out of shape.

basket weave tubes used for woven designs. They have both a smooth and a ribbed side, which pipe wide stripes.

drop flower tubes are the easiest to use and produce small flower shapes, either plain or swirled.

leaf tubes have a 'V' opening and are used to pipe leaves with pointy ends.

ruffle tubes have a teardrop tip, and are used to pipe bows, ribbons, scallops and ruffles.

rose tubes have an opening that is wide at one end and narrow at the other. It's not only used for piping roses – daisies, carnations, pansies, etc, may also be piped with this tube.

round tubes used for outlining details, filling and writing. Also piping dots, balls, beads and filigree, etc.

star tubes used to pipe shells, stars, rosettes and flowers.

PIZZA CUTTER used to cut through ready-made icing. The blade presses down vertically, rather than dragging, through the icing, which gives a clean, sharp cut.

PLUNGER CUTTERS have a plunger on top: push to cut the shape, then push to release the cut shape. Doesn't damage the shape as it pushes it out.

POWDERS AND DUSTS also known as petal, pearl, sparkles, blossom tints and lustres.

QUILTING TOOLS also known as tailor's or stitching wheels. Used to create 'stitches' on ready-made icing. Wheels are removable so the stitching can be of different lengths.

RAISINS dried sweet grapes.

RASPBERRIES known as the 'king of the berries'; cylinder-shaped, about 1.5cm-2cm long, with a deep red colour and a sweet flavour. Are fragile and spoil rapidly, so check for mildew when buying. Also available frozen.

READY-MADE ICING also known as ready-to-roll icing (RTR), fondant icing, sugar paste, plastic icing and soft icing. Is sweet tasting, and has a dough-like consistency when kneaded. Is used to cover cakes and make decorations. Roll on a surface dusted lightly with cornflour; don't use too much cornflour, as the icing will dry and crack when lifted over the cake.

ROLLING PINS come in a variety of sizes; use large ones to roll out the icing, use medium and smaller ones to thin out icing for decorations. They can be made of wood, granite, non-stick plastic, etc.

ROYAL ICING is a mixture of egg white and pure icing sugar. Pure icing sugar has no softener (cornflour) so it sets very hard. Do not use icing sugar mixture or soft icing sugar for this. Is the best to use when securing cakes to their boards. Instant mixes (just add water) are available from cake decorating suppliers.

SCRAPERS can be either plastic or metal (stainless steel). Used to scrape excess ganache off the side of a cake, or to remove excess royal icing off stencils. Plastic scrapers are useful when cleaning up, to scrape any leftover icing stuck to the bench top.

SKEWERS are used in cake decorating to support the cake tiers, they are not the same as the skewers used in kebabs, etc. They are much thicker so they are able to support the weight of the cakes stacked above. They are pointed at one end to push all the way through the cake, before cutting down to size.

SMOOTHERS plastic paddles with handles that are used to smooth ready-made icing, and remove air bubbles after the icing has been positioned on the cake. When smoothing the icing you need to use the two plastic paddles together; they give the cake a smooth, shiny, appearance.

STAMENS (the reproductive part of the flower, usually found in the centre). Most often sold double-ended, which are either cut in half before using, or are pulled through a hooked wire and folded up in a bunch. May also be found single-ended. Used to make flower centres.

STYROFOAM a tightly-packed polystyrene foam that resists moisture. Available in different-shaped blocks from cake decorating and craft stores.

SUGAR

brown a very soft, fine sugar retaining molasses for its flavour.

caster also known as superfine or finely granulated table sugar.

icing also known as confectioners' sugar or powdered sugar; granulated sugar crushed together with a small amount of added cornflour.

pure icing this sugar is also known as confectioners' sugar or powdered sugar, but it has no cornflour added; this means it is very lumpy and it has to be sifted well before use.

white a coarse, granulated table sugar, also known as crystal sugar.

SUGAR SYRUP is brushed all over the surface of a cake before applying the initial covering of ganache, almond paste or ready-made icing. It sticks the initial covering layer to the cake and sticks the final layer to the initial layer. It also stops the cake from drying out. It may be flavoured with alcohol, if you like.

TEXTURED MATS see embossing tools.

TYLOSE POWDER when mixed into royal icing, almond paste, ready-made icing or modelling paste, tylose powder creates a strong paste that dries very hard. Used when something is required to set in a certain position.

VANILLA

bean the tiny black seeds impart a luscious vanilla flavour.

extract made by extracting the flavour from the vanilla bean pods.

paste made from vanilla pods and contains real seeds. 1 teaspoon replaces a whole vanilla pod without mess or fuss as you neither have to split or scrape the pod.

VEINING TOOL also known as a leaf veiner. Plastic moulds that leave an imprint of a leaf when pressed on ready-made icing. Available in kits along with matching flower petal cutters.

WOODEN DOWELS or dowel rods, are used to support cakes over three tiers so they can be carried and transported safely. Cut with a small hacksaw to the size required (just below the height of the cake).

INDEX

Published by Bauer Media Books, a division of
Bauer Media Pty Ltd, 54 Park St, Sydney;
GPO Box 4088, Sydney, NSW 2001, Australia.
phone +61 2 9282 8618; fax +61 2 9267 3702
www.awwcookbooks.com.au

MEDIA GROUP

Published and Distributed in the United Kingdom by
Octopus Publishing Group
Endeavour House
189 Shaftesbury Avenue
London WC2H 8JY
United Kingdom
phone (+44)(0)207 632 5400
fax (+44)(0)207 632 5405
info@octopusbooks.co.uk
www.octopusbooks.co.uk

BAUER MEDIA BOOKS
Publisher Jo Runciman
Editorial & food director Pamela Clark
Director of sales, rights & marketing Brian Cearnes
Creative director Hieu Chi Nguyen
Art director Hannah Blackmore
Senior editor Julie Collard
Designer Mary Keep
Senior business analyst Rebecca Varela
Operations manager David Scotto

Printed in China

A CIP record for this book is available from the British Library.

ISBN 978-1-90977-023-2

© Bauer Media Pty Ltd 2013

Photographer Dean Wilmot
Stylist Vivien Walsh
Cake decorators Adam Cremona, Emma Braz, Nadia French,
Nicole Dicker
Decorators' assistants Michelle Boghos, Nicole Artsetos,
Charlotte Binns-McDonald

The publishers would like to thank the following for props:
Wild Lotus Floral Design www.wildlotusflorist.com.au;
Waterford Wedgwood www.wwrd.com.au

To order books
phone +44 (0)1903 828 503 or
order online at www.octopusbooks.co.uk

Send recipe enquiries to:
recipeenquiries@bauer-media.com.au

First published in 2013.
This edition published in 2015.

ALSO FROM THE BEST-SELLING COOKERY SERIES OF ALL TIME

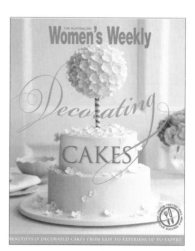

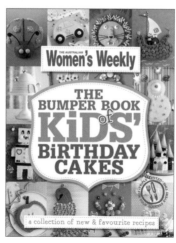

To order books visit www.octopusbooks.co.uk or telephone +44 (0)1903 828 503